The Yellow Pinto

Copyright ©2023 B.WalterWill

To request permissions, contact read@theyellowpinto.com

First paperback edition: September 2023

ISBN: 979-8-9886026-2-0

Edited By: Kristen Weber at Kevin Anderson and Associates

Cover Art: Hillary Monroy & Gianna Rose

Cover Design: Hillary Monroy

Though the book is fiction, much of this story is based on real events and experiences from my life. The situations and perceptions are my own.

Covering a series of episodic adventures, *The Yellow Pinto* follows my journey through addiction, broken relationships, and debauchery as I struggle for redemption. Unlike alcoholism or drug addiction, gambling addiction garners far less empathy. It's seen as a glamorous problem, not a disease for which one can receive treatment. And it certainly does not inspire the same heroic stories of overcoming the odds as those other, better understood diseases. Nevertheless, it is a part of the many intertwined stories that I share in *The Yellow Pinto*.

B. Walter Will

The Yellow Pinto

The meter on the dashboard clicked over to $480, more than the cost of my plane ticket. It was practically all the cash I had left to my name. But that's the cost of a ride from Yarmouth in Cape Cod to Logan Airport in Boston.

We were to be married two days later. We were supposed to be married twice before. But we'll get to that later; this time I was gone for good!

It was Christmas. The wedding was going to be giant. My fiancé was the only daughter and lone heir to a family fortune, she was absolutely gorgeous. Yeah, *that* gorgeous. I almost never recovered.

We had gotten into an argument about which artist was more influential, Prince, Bowie, The Clash, NWA… I know it's a tough choice. She would argue just to argue, she liked fights. But the day was not supposed to start with the two of us barking at each other. We were supposed to be at a beautiful Christmas dinner with all the family, colleagues, and her friends, and we had plenty to talk about.

I had flown into Boston two days earlier. Tula, my fiancé, and her friend Erin came to pick me up at the airport. We went to a Celtics game and hung out at a few dive bars, watching live music, eating great Italian food, and then driving back to Yarmouth the next day.

The check engine light in the car was on, so when we gassed up, I decided to change the oil. But after about 40 minutes into our drive in Tula's maid of honor Erin's brand-new convertible, we began smelling smoke before it began to shoot out from under the hood.

We pulled over immediately, got out, and ran! About 15 seconds later, the car was engulfed in flames, and then it exploded!

I had put the oil in the wrong spot, probably where the steering column or transmission fluid goes…

Fuck! They all looked the same to me; I should have been patient and waited for someone to help. It seemed routine and it was a task I had performed many times before. But my ego damn near killed all of us. Luckily, no one was injured and it ended up being just a funny story about my stupidity for Tula and Erin's friends back on the Cape.

When we visited Cape Cod or Mountain Lake near Belvedere, we learned that one lake was for the families who had summer homes there. The other lake, legend has it, is where the dead bodies were dumped by gangsters. It wasn't far from the George Washington Bridge.

We would always spend a few nights in the big cities of New York and Boston. I had a friend who played for the Red Sox, and for a minute, he was the toast of the town.

When we went to watch baseball, or when we had friends who played in bands we loved, we would make it a point to see them play. We had so much fun. We had great connections and got VIP treatment almost everywhere we went.

Instead of family dinner on Christmas, Tula got in an ugly, verbally demeaning argument with her mother, whom Tula loved and respected very much.

Holidays are tough for most of us – for any number of reasons; lost souls, lost friends, lost loved ones, nobody to love or give gifts to, regrets, all of it.

Tula hated her father. There was domestic abuse, and child abuse. Not to mention he gave her mom an STD while cheating on her during their marriage. He was German and had trained to be in Hitler Youth. He was a very aggressive man, a miserable husband, and a terrible father.

I am a God-fearing man who believes life is up to God's will. I believe you need to try and make an effort, but is that good enough? Does God just take life as it goes, or as we come and bring it to the deity?

Like a child, Tula threatened not to go to family dinner. She had long ago tossed her father aside. But I thought we should go; I wanted to go!

Her aunt had a gigantic mansion in Montclair, and the dinners were always spectacular. All Tula's relatives were well connected to casinos, the police department, and big time construction, and they loved to drink.

It should have been a routine event to go have dinner with Tula s family. It was Christmas after all. I liked her mother's side of the family, and we were supposed to be getting married two weeks later.

I thought I would let Tula cool off for a few hours and then we would go. I went to our room to compose myself for about an hour. When I came out, Tula was scrambling eggs, so I asked her what the hell she was doing.

"I'm making us dinner," she said.

"Why don't we go to your mom's?" I asked politely.

She turned around and whirled a frying pan full of eggs at my head. I ducked for cover, but was a little too late and the pan struck me in the back of my skull.

She had a great arm, she was a tremendous athlete and she had a better throwing arm than a lot of baseball players I'd played with. The back of my head was gashed and bleeding.

I did not say a word. I walked into our room, stuffed some things in my duffle bag, and hopped out the window. It was seven degrees below zero outside. I snuck away, leaving Tula screaming to herself in the kitchen. I walked away crying my eyes out, my tears frozen to my cheeks, while blood froze on my neck and the back of my head. With each step I took, I became more brave.

It was a fifteen-minute walk to the liquor store about a half mile away. There was a pay phone there. I bought a fifth of Jim Beam and a tall Budweiser. I had a swallow of bourbon and slammed the beer. Then I called a taxi, waited ten minutes, took another swig of bourbon and, I was gone.

With blood and tears caked to my head and face, I boarded a flight back to San Diego. And just like that, it was over. It was not the first time or the first incident. It almost never is.

It started as a dare. The first time I ever saw Tula was at the pool at a private country club hotel where my brother and I had snuck in. There is not a hotel pool or country club in any major city that I haven't snuck into. This includes the time when the President was at the Beverly Hills Hotel and I almost got caught by the Secret Service. I tore my rotator cuff jumping over the wall; there were rips all the way down the side of my back from my shoulder through the skin.

Tula was the most beautiful woman I'd ever seen in a bathing suit and my brother agreed. We had our music box blaring and positioned ourselves a few chairs down from her so we could stare.

I figured I would play something cool so she would notice so I put in The Damned. The next thing you know, she was standing in front of me.

"Hey, I know those guys!" she said.

"You know Captain Sensible, Rat Scabies, and David Vanian?" I asked in amazement.

"Yeah, my ex was a road manager for them," she said nonchalantly in a Boston accent.

"I know this great band playing tonight," I said. "I'm on the list plus one. Do you want to go?" I asked.

She immediately said yes.

We were off and running.

I shouldn't admit this, but drinking and driving was never something I worried about; it was the same for most people I knew. As long as we weren't blackout drunk, we drove. I wish we'd known better, but we did it all the time; all my friends did it, everybody I knew did it. Even the parents we knew did it. We lost some dear friends to it…in some real bad accidents and horrible tragedies.

One tragic incident involved a guy named Burt who was driving to see his new son. Burt got hit by another person in a head-on collision with a guy named Pete who was shitfaced drunk and driving on the wrong side of the road. He was speeding on his way to see the girl he'd gotten pregnant. Burt never had a chance. He died instantly, was declared brain dead, and the plug was pulled. He never got a chance to meet his baby girl and hold her in his arms.

The baby's mother was a girl he'd had a tumultuous relationship with; they had made amends. Earlier, she used me to get my brother and whoever she was dating at the time jealous. She was notorious for giving hickies everywhere, among other talents like breaking up relationships.

Pretty much all of us were young, immature, curious, and stupid.

I hit my first home run over a fence in Little League off Burt. My dad's colleague and friend gave me a transistor radio as a reward.

I woke up once next to a girl after we'd passed out after having sex on ice plant on a hill next to my apartment. We went into my apartment to have more sex then sleep it off. She left her new convertible Mustang at my house and she was gone the next morning when I woke up.

My friend Cole and I went back to the same bar where we met the girl every night for almost two weeks, it was our regular spot. We'd drive her car, figuring it wouldn't be reported stolen because the cops would have found it in our parking lot, so we drove it before she finally showed up.

My friend Cole and I were shooting pool on "Let's smash bottles and pee in the alley night" [girls included] when suddenly, a voice shouted over the loud vintage punk music.

"Got my keys?" She appeared out of nowhere. "I'm engaged and live with my fiancé," she said. "I told him I scraped the wall with my car door, and it was at the body shop, not that I was fucking your brains out."

"That you did, my dear," I said. "Nice meeting you."

I never saw her again, and I don't remember her name.

Tula looked amazing when I picked her up at the condo her parents had bought for her. She was wearing a black mini, with high black pumps and a gold chain around her ankle.

We split a six-pack of Budweiser while she spun records of bands I had never heard before. Limited edition shit, it was fabulous. She introduced me to a lot of new bands and a lot of new films that I had never seen or heard before; it was her biggest gift to me.

We never left the condo. We drank all the booze she had, and the next thing I knew, I was head first between her legs for an hour before she let me fuck her. It was glorious!

And just like that, we were together. Inseparable. And we had a routine. God, I was in love, lust, awe, all of the above with her. I was delirious.

Our routine was pretty simple. We'd drink beer for a bit, go to a bar, and watch a few bands, then come home and fuck like animals. Or we would go for a swim or a hike. She was much faster than I was; she was in better condition. Then we'd come home and ravage each other.

All the guys would gawk at her, but I didn't mind. She would occasionally flirt with a few of the band members, but what could I say? I flirted with the waitresses at the bars where we were regulars and at the ones we weren't. It's healthy. It's second nature to want and be wanted.

Once, a lead singer fell on our table and bled on her. He was completely covered in blood and sweat. He climbed up to the ceiling and just swan dived on the table. Tula wore it and viewed it as a badge of honor.

She had crazy sex appeal and a curiosity in her eyes, but she wasn't obvious. She was almost oblivious to her beauty. But she had it! And she knew it. She never had to try to look gorgeous.

We would occasionally fight over which band was better live, but that was about it. Politically, we were pretty much on the same page. We were both earth conscious and she taught me a lot about the environment. We were cool. Then…

It was pouring rain one night, and we'd both had one too many cocktails. She'd probably had three too many. She could hold her liquor but we all have tipping points. The extra two shots of Jim Beam weren't necessary.

We were driving home and she changed the song. I probably should have let it go, it was one of her friend's bands from Boston and I had a feeling maybe he was an ex, but maybe not.

Not even 20 seconds into the song, I said, "This is horseshit!"

"Fuck you," she said.

I changed the song while speeding down the freeway in the pouring rain.

She took her left leg and reached over and hit the brakes hard! We spun around several times and landed in an embankment. The airbags deployed.

The car was stuck in the mud on the side of a mountain. It was a total wreck and Tula clawed her way out. I was stuck in the seat with the airbag draped over me.

There were several empty beer containers on the floor in the back, but I had to move fast in case the cops came. By the way thank God and thank Jesus we were both OK.

I wiggled out of the vehicle my dad had loaned me, or quid pro quod me, and Tula was walking away. What was she going to do, walk home?

She was wearing short jean shorts, high heels, and a leather jacket. With her long blonde hair, she couldn't have looked any better in the rain.

I got rid of the beer cans by tossing them up the hill behind some bushes. Then, I started after her. As soon as she saw me, she stuck her thumb out. She was a good quarter mile ahead of me.

Wouldn't you know the first semi that pulled by, she was crawling in, then she was gone.

I was stuck, like a dumb shit in the rain, with a wrecked car. What to do? But it only took 20 minutes to land a ride. The savior of a semi-truck driver dropped me close to our house.

We lived down a curvy street that would have been hard for any skilled truck driver to navigate. I flipped him a $20 bill, thanked him, and got out and walked towards Tula's condo.

It was locked and she wasn't opening up. I pounded the door for about ten minutes to no avail. Then I decided to get creative. I climbed on top of her car and hoisted myself onto the balcony to open the sliding glass door into her bedroom. The door was already open. I walked in and yelled, "Where are you?"

Then there she was, surrounded by candlelight in the bathtub.

"What took you so long?" she asked. "Climb in."

■ ■

Th

It wasn't the first time I'd wrecked a car, and it was the start of me wrecking this and many later relationships.

Bad habits ignored catch up with you eventually. I developed one, maybe two, probably many more bad habits.

The first car I drove was a clunker stick shift. I was 15, and my dad taught me how to drive. It was an early lesson on running bets to the racetrack or the bookie and/or an organized family and neighborhood friend.

I learned to drive on a dirt road. My dad took me there so that if I wrecked or sputtered the car, I wouldn't hurt anyone. It was a road with tons of memories. It connected the inland of San Diego to the beach of Del Mar. It was barely five miles long and sparsely populated by mansions and compounds in Rancho Santa Fe.

When we were too broke to spend money in bars or during summers in college when our fake IDs didn't work, or we just wanted to get away from home or have somewhere to go chat with friends or hook up, we would party on that stretch of road over campfires. Sometimes we would have huge gatherings there and anyone could come.

Monique and I were forbidden from seeing each other. It was our first year out of college and we'd met at a rave club, started making out, then she snuck me into her room. We would spend many nights and days on that dirt road learning a lot about sex and each other.

I thought it would be cool to drop out of college and baseball to try being a singer in a punk rock band. College was never really a priority for Monique; she had a part time job as a waitress in a hotel. The bartender would hook us up with these crazy cocktail concoctions and we would go and get sloppy and sexy together. Then she got pregnant.

Her mom kept telling her she was too young to have a baby. My parents really did not know what to do at the time. My mom is a staunch Catholic, and my dad just yelled at me to keep my head out of my ass and wear a rubber. It was a touch and go situation.

Monique wanted the baby, and I told her I would be there and help and support her. I was in love with her and thought that was more than enough. After a few weeks of going back and forth, then a few days where she didn't talk to me at all, she terminated the pregnancy and our relationship. Just like that, we were done.

She called me a week later from Indiana and told me her mother had made her do it. She'd flown Monique to Indiana to stay with her aunt and to start her life over again. Monique's mother wanted to get her away from any possibility of us getting back together.

I had won a little bit of money gambling and saved a little more from a job I had pumping gas and fixing flat tires. I called Monique and told her I would fly her back and we could get a cheap hotel room and get back together. That is exactly what happened, and our first four days were blissful. Then we thought we'd would take the dirt road again and go to the beach.

Her aunt had covered for her to her mom, and my mom just thought I was out screwing around with friends. We stopped at the liquor store and got some wine coolers for the day at the beach. In the car, Monique's head was busy on my lap after drinking a second wine cooler when out of nowhere, a Mercedes Benz parked on our side of the road up decided to do a sudden u-turn directly at us. Instinctively, I pulled Monique off my lap before the collision and she crashed through the windshield, me still clutching the back of her head with one arm, and the other bending the steering wheel. Her face was a bloody mess; she'd sliced her forehead open.

I had the presence of mind to get rid of the wine coolers before the cops arrived. Monique was okay except for her forehead and a minor concussion. I was just sore. The lady in the Benz was fine. The Mercedes is a tank, especially against a little compact Chevy hatchback.

It was 100 percent the other woman's fault. She admitted she never looked when she pulled out. Because of the blood and head trauma, Monique was airlifted to the hospital and her mother was called. The cat was out of the bag and both our families knew we were seeing each other again.

Her mother immediately warned me to keep my distance. She spoke with my mom who agreed. Reluctantly, Monique headed back to Indiana and I thought we'd never see each other again.

It would be two years later when I stopped into a coffee shop in San Clemente that I would see Monique at the counter. She waited on me. She had met someone in Indiana and had to get away from him; she was a single mother. We saw each other a few more times, but it was time for both of us to grow up and move on.

∎∎

The

It's a habit that breaks a lot of families, relationships, and trust. They won't let you in the baseball Hall of Fame because of it although they allow far worse crimes. So does society. It's why my mom left my dad. It's an addiction that has also brought me some of my fondest memories with my dad and in my life. It has also brought me some of my greatest pains.

Tula and I were going to go on a cross country drive together, and I wanted to go the southern route so I could show her New Orleans. As an added bonus, I could stop in Kentucky afterwards to see the Breeders Cup. A group of $1,000,000 purse horse races that happens once a year.

I didn't tell Tula.

The Fairgrounds Racetrack was in New Orleans, which Tula didn't know yet. I was always in and out of money. I made up a lot of lies to excuse myself.

There we were in a little sports car, stuffed with a kitten that we'd adopted and had to bottle feed, a Pomeranian, a ferret, and two more cats I was definitely allergic to. Not two hours into our trip another argument broke out about the playlist.

Please understand, my dad got me my first car because the dirt road led through Rancho Santa Fe and into Del Mar. We would pass by the Ray Kroc McDonald's mansion and all the mansions on the way to Del Mar. This was pre-satellite wagering, and my dad would like to drive to the track itself to get a bet down. Then you could stay and watch, or listen by phone as the race was called. Or later, you could hear the results on the radio. If you stayed at the race track, you could also get paid immediately when you cashed your ticket. Bookies only meet once a week to settle up payments, hoping and banking that you'll lose back what money was won.

Even the major news stations would broadcast the stretch call of every race every 15 minutes on the hour. Tula was under the impression I was fascinated by the news.

You always knew who the sickos were. When they looked at their cell phones constantly or ran to a pay phone to get the results. My favorite was being overly interested in listening or watching the news, waiting to hear the race results or scores.

My job after school and during my lunch break was to run my dad's bets to the track while he was at work. A 15-year-old boy running bets not old enough to have a license.

This is where the fight over the radio began, only this time I placed the bet in the town we were leaving at some Indian casino.

"Let's hear the news on the radio now," I said to Tula. Usually it came on every 30 minutes so you could time it.

"I want music now," she said and changed the station.

Keep in mind my allergies were going nuts in the animal shelter wagon. I tried to turn on the news and a fight broke out.

"I cannot take any more of this rolling animal shelter!" I said. "Leave me here."

Screech...

Tula kicked me out of the car in the middle of nowhere with no phone. After about 20 minutes, I heard repeated honking. She came back and picked me up and the trip continued.

I have two brothers; we all got along fine. We've always been like best friends. One time my grandfather overheard us bickering, going back and forth to my mom about who was doing what to whom. He took the three of us aside, lined us up, and slapped us each on the face once hard, but not too hard. Then he proclaimed in his Spanish accent, "You are brothers. You are best friends. You cover each other's backs and never let any of this bullshit get back to your mom."

I was the oldest, and my dad and mom would let me know all of our family secrets including everything about our financials, our relatives, or anything else, but I always had to keep these things from my brothers.

When I was about twelve years old, my father had a favorite horse he wanted to see run live. It was his excuse to gamble, and my mom didn't want to go; she said they couldn't afford it. The two of them would occasionally go away to Santa Anita or Hollywood Park for a few days to get away for some peace, quiet, and sanity from me and my brothers, and also probably have some honeymoon time. Hence, my younger sister. But this time, my dad brought me, a 12-year-old kid, and it was a wonderful day.

The place was massive and packed full of characters ranging from loudmouth cigar blowers trying to hustle "expert" picks (there's no such thing), as well as escorts, degenerate gamblers and Kings and Queens. It is called The Sport of Kings for a reason.

So I walked with my dad to the betting window to bet his horse. I had $12 in allowance money in my pocket from babysitting and other little odd jobs, I gave it to my dad to bet on the 9 horse for me.

The race went off. We were squeezed into the stands and the place was going bananas! It was a Graded Stake Race and lots of money was on the line. The two horses were neck and neck coming down the stretch, all the way down to the wire, the 4 and the 9. It was a photo finish; no one could tell who had won. The fans were even with a 50/50 split, and they posted the 9 up first.

Then the announcer announced that the jockey of the 4 horse was claiming a foul, and said the 9 bumped him repeatedly. But after a ten-minute review, they left the 9 horse up and I had won. I was hooked.

Little did Tula know that our trips and stopovers were planned at stops that had a race tracks or a place where I could put down any type of wager. Little did I know her aunt and uncle owned parts of two casinos in New Jersey.

Tula caught on in New Orleans, and Kentucky was a blast. I was winning and we were partying our asses off everywhere. We stayed in the best hotels. We had unlimited bar tabs. We ate and drank wherever and whatever we wanted. We were so fucking happy!

We humped like rabbits all the time. When she recommended I start taking Claritin, even the pets didn't bother my allergies anymore.

Her family owned several places from the Virgin Islands, to La Jolla, to Montclair, to Belvedere, to New York City, to downtown Boston, to Cape Cod, and on and on. We stopped at her Grandma's place on the lake just over the George Washington Bridge in New Jersey and I learned a valuable lesson. Her grandma was making sandwiches and she wanted to know if I wanted a certain type of meat. Tula stepped in and said, "He doesn't eat that." It was ham and she claimed I didn't eat it because of the nitrates, but Tula loved pepperoni pizza. Funny how rules only apply at certain times.

Her grandma uttered this very important credo, "Don't let your appetite become his appetite and vice versa, and don't apologize for it!" There was nothing to apologize for.

My mom eventually left my dad because of gambling, despite how much she loved him. He left us broke, bankrupt, and with no home. He had lost all of it. He also left my mom with terrible credit, and a tax bill over $200,000. She was so broke she had to jog to a rent-a-wreck to rent a car. Back then, the rent-a-wreck made you bring the car back to them if your credit was bad, then they would check it back out in the morning. I remember one morning it was raining so hard that she had to run in the rain to get the car so she could drive to work an hour away.

When I was younger, the Giancarlo Sisters would take turns babysitting us. They would play cool music and drink our mom and dad's booze, and talk on the phone a lot. We swore we would never tell and we never did. They were like goddesses and we would just stare at them. They even would bring their bathing suits and lay out on weekends if our parents went out together for the day or on a mini vacation. We would ask them stupid questions and just gawk at them, whether we were at their home pool or in our backyard patches of grass.

They also brought their kid brother Louie with them. Louie was flamboyantly gay and not really into sports. We liked him a lot because he knew a lot about women, or so it seemed. We were clueless, and he would always have girls over to play.

Louie had a huge impact on us as 10 and 11-year-olds. The girls loved him because he was pretty, plus he would make the girls play spin the bottle with us even though we were goofballs. It was him they wanted to kiss, and he did. Louie showed us how to French kiss, and the game had a two minutes in heaven section if you landed on the person twice in a row. You would just go off to the side and feel each other up. What a summer it was. Louie was quite popular.

We remained friends through college, keeping in touch occasionally. His dad died a mysterious death; the report was his body was found washed ashore after going missing for a few weeks. Our parents were good friends; they were a close-knit crew. They would go on vacations and out on the town frequently together.

A few years later we ran into each other at a gay nightclub. The gay nightclubs were notoriously great for after hours, speakeasys, and drugs. I was straight and had gay friends but never felt unwelcome any time I went to these clubs. I usually brought girls, and avoided anyone who might be prejudiced toward anyone for whatever reason. I did not care what anyone thought about me for going to those clubs. I was happy to see Louie so happy, not having to hide the fact that he was gay.

It made me comfortable that he was comfortable, and vice versa.

The Y

I was left to help raise my sister. It is amazing how much a man can learn from women and about women by helping to raise a loved one, in this case my sister. In many ways I was truly clueless.

Girls grow up faster than boys. It's that simple. I think it's because they can find trouble easier than boys. Think about this: how many senior girls do you see with freshman or sophomore boys? In my experience, in high school almost every girl I was interested in was with someone older. I saw it every painful day on campus. My sister was about fourteen when she and her friends somehow got a hold of fake IDs – probably from some of her friends' sisters in college – and decided to ditch school for the day.

I got a phone call from a bartender. He had my sister and her four friends drunk off their asses, I was told I better get there fast or he was going to call the police because he and the staff did not want to babysit them.

When I arrived, I looked at the five of them and thanked him for giving me a heads up. "I'll get them out of here," I told him. My ex fiancé Julia who was nicknamed Big

Red, and myself dragged them to the car one at a time. They could barely walk, and two of them threw up in the parking lot near the beach. Jesus Christ! "You guys went a little overboard don't ya think?" I said.

They were dressed like hookers, with makeup smeared everywhere and they smelled like they swam in a pool of perfume. They were a mess.

The manager called because he saw a few of the girls were zealously making out with older men and he got suspicious. He asked what astrology sign they were and then had them show him their IDs. None of them had a clue. One of the IDs was for a girl in her late thirties. He said it was laughable.

He admonished the door man and took pity on me because he said he had a younger sister himself. He mentioned that it happens all the time but usually it's when the club gets too crowded. The middle of the day is usually an older, working class/attire, happy hour crowd. These girls stuck out more than the pineapples and celery sticks garnishing their drinks.

I called the girls' parents and let them know they were studying for a mid-term school project and that they would be staying the night at our house. I spoke with the girls and warned them of the potential dangers of being too drunk and what could happen to them in a compromised condition. I promised all of them I would not tell their parents or my mother. Big Red and I made them some soup and put them to bed and that was that.

As spectacular as this trip was with Tula, she was getting hip to me. We were supposed to get married two different times, once in San Francisco. Instead we did acid with friends the night before and changed our minds the next day because a we couldn't find a chapel and we were too hungover. The two of us were completely spun out of our minds, driving in circles up and down the steep hill streets of the city, totally dizzy and lost to common sense. We went back to the house where we took a shower and had sex off and on for hours. Then we fell asleep looking at portraits of dogs dressed like humans.

The other time was in La Jolla. Instead of going to Tijuana to get married we ended up going to the beach, found a secret spot and brought a picnic basket with a flask of sangria, grapes, and dry crusted Italian salami. Then we made love at sunset until sunrise in a very private spot south. It was a beautiful experience we had together.

The longer we dated, the more Tula became irritated that I really did not have a secure stream of income. But don't kid yourself, gambling is a full-time job and mistress…and nerve wrecker.

Tula worked her pussy off as an assistant for a veterinarian for very little money. Despite her family's wealth, she was always employed. She loved animals and loathed lazy people.

We planned a wedding because I saved my hide by getting hired at a brokerage, then getting my Series 7 license. I was doing very well. I was getting paid too because I brought in a few wealthy clients on my journeys out and about at restaurants and bars.

I wasn't doing well enough, however, when I found out that a recently divorced woman I brought in to the brokerage was a real big fish, and the firm made a fortune on the commission. I was rewarded with an envelope of two thousand dollars, and two escorts that had been arranged for me. Regardless, it looked like I had a bright future.

Tula worked at Scripps Ranch, and at the time, was nursing a very expensive broodmare whose rear leg was injured. The mare had to be harnessed so she wouldn't put any pressure on the leg; it would be fatal if she did. She was a longshot to recover; most horses would just be put down.

I used Tula's car to drop her off and go to school or work, then I'd sneak off to the track. When I got back to the barn to pick up Tula, I would help, shit, piss, and feed the broodmare. Sometimes we would be there for hours until the vet got there. Nursing that injured broodmare was a full-time event.

I must honestly say it was truly God's work, and then it happened again late that night. Tula and I had a few beers while we were waiting for the vet to show up. Then we had another stupid argument on the drive out of the ranch, and this time Tula decided to put her leg over and stomp on the gas pedal. Maybe she was going for the brakes again, but we slammed smack into 100-year-old eucalyptus tree. It was not pretty.

The car was totaled, but we somehow walked away with minor injuries; just a few bruises. The vet graciously drove us home.

Now I'm not a masochist, and I am not crying domestic abuse, although I probably could have. I reserve that for those cases that are truly warranted. Maybe I was one of them and just didn't know it. Sooner or later you would think enough was enough, and after a while you'd move on. The iceberg was tipping before the wedding.

About a month before, I decided I would try skiing with her in the Poconos Mountains. I was no slouch as an athlete myself. I'd had a full ride baseball scholarship before I got kicked out of college for gambling, but Tula was a world class athlete at anything she tried. Only my brother Antonio was as talented as she was. Little did I know that Tula was damn near an Olympic-level slalom skier. Who would think a swimmer would be great skier? I should have known since she was raised in Stuttgart, Germany on the ski slopes.

"We will start down the peewee slope," she said. It should be noted that my baseball career ended a little after my expulsion on another full ride scholarship. It happened when I was involved in a vicious home plate collision on a drizzly and windy day. I tore my knee ligaments and cartilage so badly that my shin was dangling from my thigh.

I like about any weather except Arizona heat in the summer when it's 100 degrees plus every day, but I have never been fond of the wind.

I managed to cajole myself down the slope a few times, but I was barely hanging on for dear life. I could not wait to get Tula back to the lodge jacuzzi to get her naked and start drinking.

She thought it would be fun if I tried the double black diamond expert slope with her. She had done a few runs easily, she said while I was puttering down the beginner slope.

It was snowing and blustery and she went first, making it look easy. Then it was my turn.

At full speed I completely wiped out, leaving bits and pieces of myself all the way down the hill while Tula stood at the bottom, crying with laughter. I lost my ski poles and one of my boots. It was as ugly and bad as an accident can get.

I was fucking embarrassed and yelled at her. "How would you like it if I threw fastballs at your head to teach you how to hit a baseball?" I yelled. "Does that sound fun?" I looked down and realized I'd lost a ski. "Fuck the ski I lost up the hill," I said. "I'm not hiking all the way back up, and fuck my deposit too." I was battered and bruised.

"Wait here," she said.

She took the trolley back up and skied down the hill and found my lost boot, pole, and ski. She then dropped me off at the lodge and set me up at the bar. I was on my second whiskey when she returned and apologized. It was a nice gesture.

We got to the room and made love like it was our wedding night. She got pregnant from that time I'm sure of it. Later in the relationship she would have a miscarriage.

5:00am came and she wanted to go back to the slopes. I wasn't happy with the wakeup call. I hate early mornings to begin with, but I went along at the crack of sunlight.

"I've had enough," I said.

"Fine, then pitch me fucking baseballs," she said. Was she kidding?

No.

We had a bat and some tennis balls, and a few baseballs scattered in the trunk from a few months back when I thought it be fun to teach her how to hit a baseball.

I was still hungover and deliriously happy from the night before. I asked again, "Are you serious?"

"Let's go!" she said.

I didn't throw a strike. Every pitch, every ball was at her body, and I hit her not once, but twice. I head hunted with the tennis balls, and scared her with the hardballs. I got a few body shots in as well, and then I accidentally nailed her in her beautiful thigh with the hardball. She was in pain.

She threw her bat down and cried, "I give up! We're going home. Let's pack our shit and get the hell out of here."

Love makes you crazy; it makes you do stupid, preposterous things.

Later in my life while I was on a metro bus that was completely packed, two gay guys snuck on through the back door. I was standing next to them and each of them had hickeys all over their necks. I began to notice something moving inside one of their zip-up leather jackets. Out fell an animal leg. A puppy? A bigger dog? It was a pig! A baby snort-nosed pig. The guy had to unzip his jacket because the pig was scratching to get out and he wasn't wearing a t-shirt.

They got off at the next stop. I thought, *my gosh that is true love…*

■■■

The Ye

My mom hung up the phone and came running toward me. I entered with two girls and some friends who were with other girls and a bottle of Jägermeister. It would be the first time I heard the news. When I came through the door, I heard, "You stupid asshole!" My mom welcomed me at the top of her voice. It is always a date with trauma when a gambling/addict is concerned.

My mother had the phone in her hand as she ran to me and then started beating me over the head with it. "Didn't you learn enough from your dad?" she asked.

I was kicked out of college, and had my baseball scholarship revoked. I was getting by okay in school, however I was having a great winter season in baseball preparing for the spring. I was really getting good and maturing physically. I had been a bit of a late bloomer growing up.

I remember Shannon when I was about 12 or 13 years old. She would always meet me in the middle of the day wearing short denim cutoffs with her long beautiful tan legs with peach fuzz on the thighs. We would make out and do pretty much everything else except sex. I had not started

puberty yet, and rumor was she was going out with some senior baseball player named Ron.

The best players of my age were brought up to work out with the varsity baseball team at the end of the year; it was a big honor. I was one of them. When I walked into the men's locker room, it was a big awakening. I was a boy against men. I gave up Shannon immediately.

In college, I was probably the team's best player. In addition, I was probably one of the better hitters in the United States. We had two future major leaguers on our roster.

I never thought I would get kicked out of college because of my ability in baseball. I was warned not once, but pleaded with twice. But how did they know I was gambling? Other players on my team wagered on football games. They had bookies and they openly bet with everybody. They were very vocal about it.

Stupid mistake number one. This mistake became very real because a very good friend of mine on the baseball team told me a very big secret in extreme confidence. His brother was the offensive coordinator of a major college football team in the Southeast Conference. Mikey was a great guy and everybody loved him. Later on, he would own a few successful bars on Bourbon Street, he became a big executive on the gambling board for the riverboat casinos. He also loved to gamble, and so did our coach. I found out later other coaches did too. Little did I know our baseball coach's brother was the biggest bookie/bookmaker in the state.

In addition to my ignorant bliss, I didn't know that my phone was being tapped. Mikey told me that his brother the offensive coordinator had gave him some information about an upcoming football game. This was the best information anybody could ever get. His brother's team was favored to win the game by 40 points. He told me they would win the game easy, but definitely not cover the 40-point spread. This is referred to as point shaving.

I called everyone I knew back home, including my dad. I told them to wager the underdog, take the 40 points. I didn't say why, but I told them to trust me.

"No way," I heard. "That team they're playing is terrible."

"Just trust me," I reassured them.

The game began, and at halftime, Mikey's brother's team was already winning 42 to 0.

Everybody started calling me, screaming at me, worried sick about the bets they had placed. To be honest, I was a bit worried too.

I bet what I had saved; I also bet what I didn't have on this particular game. Bookies give you a credit line.

The brother's side scored again in the third quarter to make it 49 to 0. "Oh shit, I'm fucked!" I said out loud.

Then, on the next possession, the second string of the brother's team came out on both offense and defense. A few missed tackles here, a few blunders there, a few easy touchdowns later for the other team, and the final score was Mikey's brother's team 49, underdog 17.

We all won! A lot! $25,000 is a lot of cash for a college kid.

College football games happen on a Saturday with NFL games usually on Sundays. The Monday morning after baseball workouts I was called into the office by the head baseball coach.

"I heard you had quite a weekend," he said.

I played stupid and didn't admit to anything.

"I've got good news for you and bad news for you," he continued. "The good news is, you're going to get paid. The bad news is, the bookie that you're set up with here in this state is my brother. This stops, or you're gone," he said.

I didn't believe him, and I carried on only through a different source. On weekends, my dad would run my bets. Then came my final mistake.

It was the last week before the semester break and I thought a certain team could not lose, and I bet on it. I bet what I had, leaving just a little bit left so when I got home, I could still have a great break and have fun with all my friends. I figured if I had lost a bet, I had a few weeks during the break to hustle up what I needed and pay it back.

I got on the phone again, then, like an idiot, I told everyone to bet on the team. The game looked like a certain winner, so much so that during the game I was getting updates from fellow students during the baseball game I was playing. We had it in the bag. There was no way to lose.

During the game, different classmates and bar mates were yelling the score at me. Even the multiple girls I was dating would walk by and hold up the score scribbled in their notebooks. It totally got out of control.

"Let's go celebrate! Meet us at our usual spot," I shouted back.

I went to go celebrate thinking I had already won, but when I walked in, it was worse than a funeral. Everybody had lost and lost a lot. It was a miracle victory for the other side. It was a once in a lifetime way to lose a game.

The opposing team threw a Hail Mary pass to tie the game, then in overtime while giving up a touchdown, the quarterback fumbled the ball and the opposing team ran it back for another touchdown. Simply put, our team were 12 point underdogs with a seven point lead with two seconds left to play. The opposing team tied and scored 13 points in overtime.

The administration, the coach, and the teachers had it all recorded. And I owed money. I flew home. And then my mom got the call.

And then, a few years later, my mom got the call again.

The Yel

I was in my fourth quarter of law school, about halfway to graduation. My mom was making a better life for herself after the divorce; she had started a very successful all woman health spa.

Because I was on my ass and promised to go to law school, she bought me what she could afford: a beat up old tan Honda Civic with a wooden stick shift. I was so grateful to her, and happy to not have to borrow or hitch rides.

Years later, her partner ripped her off by taking everything she had built from scratch including a lot of money, and a lot of dreams for many women who needed a place away for themselves- or from men for a variety of reasons. She would bounce back again. She always moved ahead just saying; "your health is your wealth." She always came back, and remains kind to everyone no matter what her situation is.

Had this happened to almost anyone else, they would have put the partner on a loose horse and lit a firecracker in the middle of the desert. The only way to find the body is to watch where the hawks are circling. Taking chunks of skin peck by peck…

I was on my way to my last final, when suddenly the car broke down. I hadn't been to the racetrack or gambled in months. It was a part of the deal I made with my mother for the car and occasional help she would give me. I broke down in a very dangerous spot on the freeway, and I could not get to a safe place. I pushed the car, waving off traffic on the side. I stuck my thumb out and a Yellow Pinto pulled over to pick me up.

"Need gas?" the black man asked me.

"No, that car is through," I told him.

"Well," he said, "I'm going to the casino. You want to ride along?"

I only had $42 in my pocket but I said, "Sure, let's get off this freeway exit first. I'll buy us some beers."

"Done deal," he said. "Give me a few dollars for gas and we'll be on our way."

We get to the casino, slammed the rest of the beers in the parking lot, and then went our separate ways. He went to the card tables and I went to the sports book.

I had about $26 in my pocket for the first race I bet. I'd given him ten dollars for gas and the rest for the beers. I bet $6 to win on a horse that was 40/1 odds, and he won! All of a sudden, I had close to $300.

Then came the next gamble, the pick six. It requires you to pick the winners of six consecutive races, which is very hard to do, but you can put multiple horses in each race to increase your chances of winning. But that can get very expensive. So I put in a $280 ticket, and six races later, I had turned 26 crumbs for dollars into $51,000.

I went back to the card room side of the casino and found my new friend. "Thanks for the ride," I said and put down $5000 cash in front of him with a shot of Don Julio Silver. Thank God he picked me up. He toasted me and played on.

I called my mom and told her I would not be

home for a couple days, that I had just won $51,000 at the racetrack. "You're going back to school, aren't you?" she asked.

"Of course," I said. I meant it too.

I found one of the cutest waitresses I could, and asked her if she wanted to go party. She eagerly came along. We rented a very nice hotel room, and we ordered room service and champagne for the next two days. She had connections and knew how to spend money well. A limo driver she knew took us to some upscale private places. I enjoyed myself thoroughly, but a gambler needs to gamble and it was time to find another casino and press my luck.

I called my teacher in law school, and told him I had an emergency and needed a few weeks before I'd be ready to come back. Because I was doing so well pursuing my law degree, he was accommodating.

Two weeks became three weeks, three weeks became skipping the quarter, and I never went back to law school. Instead, my first stop was the bank to withdraw cash for gambling, hotels, and chasing women. The problem was that this was becoming a daily occurrence and I was getting too close to busted again. And then the unthinkable happened.

My mom was in my head saying, "Go back to school. Go back to school, foolish boy!" All the hard work she'd done for our family, her hopes and dreams were draped on my shoulders.

There was a mandatory pay out day on the pick six, and the pool would reach millions. I put in a $1200 ticket to increase my chances. I also found out through various connections that a horse was going to get special medical attention and win, a big longshot.

A girlfriend who had a friend working for a vet, said there was a special milkshake/medicine cocktail that was untraceable. We had decided to key the horse and make it our best bet. I thought she was probably telling the truth. I decided to make a large wager on the horse.

It was true, the dope worked, the horse won easy. But I did not bet him to win. Instead, I singled him on my pick six ticket leaving me five out of seven horses to win between $500,000 to 2.5 million dollars.

Every one of the gamblers knew it because I was the Lone Ranger (the only person who used the horse on a ticket) screaming for the winner the race while the remainder of the crowd remained silent. Everyone, including the worst luck gambler known to humankind, Prince Victor. Other gamblers and horseman would give him money to bet on the other horse they did not have or scared of, just to stop them. He was worse than a Jinx.

If he liked the same horse that you did, you might as well tear up your ticket. He lost 99 percent of the time. He used to cry, "Not even God could stop me." He might have been right.

I later developed a sweet soft spot for him and would give him jelly rolls when I won. A jelly roll is $20 to $1000 depending on your winnings. It's what gamblers do to keep others going or have action, and as an act of karma I suppose.

The race began and one of my five horses was winning easy. "You got it!" he screamed.

"Don't fucking say that!" I told him. "Not until it's home past the wire."

He said it again.

I screamed back again.

Then others joined in. "Not even the Prince can stop this one; you're home!"

"Please don't say it!" I pleaded.

Then, no bullshit, about 15 yards from the wire, a seagull flew out of the air and hit the horse on the nose. The horse bolted sideways, knocking the jockey off, and one of the two horses I did not have passed by.

Prince started running before I could chase him. It was a shame, or it wasn't meant to be.

I really enjoyed learning the law. I could also say after my experience in law school and despite what many people think of lawyers… Let's be honest, it's not the most loved profession, except for when you need one.

When you're going to law school, at least 90% of the people that are there are in it for the right reason, hoping to make a difference and make the world a better place. The other 10% were unapologetic ambulance chasers, they go to a funeral passing out their business cards, or waiting at the

hospital before the victim showed up. Some lawyers even staged accidents, putting a crew together to steal a car, plant a gun or drugs, then hit and run somebody with a "clean" record and suddenly "appear" in the vacated car. The doctors would report the fake injuries. At least that's what it felt like to me, and I had no desire to represent child molesters or violent criminals.

My Uncle Frank was one of the 90%. He was very successful and a good family man, but when we were in our young teens, he taught us how to find trouble. When we visited him in San Francisco when were about 17 or 18, he drove us into work and gave us each fifty bucks and told us to beat it. "Meet me back here by 10 pm," he said.

It was the first time in the city for two dipsticks like us; we didn't know anything. What a time we had! Hustling girls on the Embarcadero, getting kicked out of bars for not being old enough, staying in a few a bars because nobody checked our age, meeting new people. We went in record stores, sex shops, and ate dumplings until we almost puked.

Time flew and it was 10pm before we knew it. We raced back to meet our uncle Frank. He took us to Fisherman's Wharf for seafood, cioppino, and Anchor Steam.

There was also the time a few years earlier when were about 15 and he told my mom we were going to the beach. We went riding for a bit, knocked over a few construction signs and orange road cones, then went off-roading on the dirt road toward the ocean. It was my uncle's mission to go to the all nude

Blacks Beach in La Jolla. It is not exactly an easy spot to get to, but finally we did.

There were naked people everywhere of both sexes. They were all ages from 18 to 90 years old, and all sizes too. We stood there with our boogieboards staring and sharing a bottle of Southern Comfort with my uncle. He disappeared for a couple of hours; he was talking to some older college girls, and we just goofed around and surfed. It was cool because our uncle trusted us enough to stay cool and mind our own business. That is just about the best life lesson that can be passed on. Enjoy the moment, observe, then act accordingly. Live your life.

During the process of making a film about strippers and trying to fund the film, once a week, Danielle (my girlfriend at the time), and I would go to the racetrack together. This drew a lot of attention. Danielle was dancing and method acting and she met a lot of girls who were very friendly. A lot of these girls also wanted to be in the film. They were gorgeous girls. And yes, we had sex with many of them. It was as good a thing going as it could get if I did not fall in love with someone else.

Danielle would say, "I do not care where your dick goes, but your mind and time are mine."

Eventually it did.

I met the love of my life, or so everyone thought, through my sister, and my sister met the love of her life through me. We met them both in different ways. I lost Danielle due to my own stupidity, infidelity, lies, and poor financial decisions.

My sister lost hers to pancreatic cancer, leaving behind a two-year-old son and an eight-year-old daughter. She had met him on a night out at a dive bar, when I noticed him watching the beat up old TV by himself. His Tennessee accent came through. I asked what he was doing looking through the fuzz and he said, "Trying to see myself" on the local cable comedy feeder. The bar was empty, then I introduced him to my sister. I am the godfather to their children.

I knew Danielle through my sister; they were in high school together. Danielle was too young to fall in love with me but she did, and when she started college we began to see each other behind the backs of my sister and my girlfriend, Julia.

Julia was nicknamed Big Red. She was a tall, gorgeous, exceptionally built redhead with whom I had a lot fun. She was loyal to a fault. We became involved in the post-gig after hours scene with many of the bands we knew.

I owe her my life. One afternoon while eating tacos and drinking beer, I began to choke. I could not breathe, and time was running out. It is fucking frightening when you cannot breathe at all and there is nothing you can do. Julia sprang up, grabbed me around my back, and performed the Heimlich Maneuver. The taco shell flew across the room and my life was saved.

Julia loved bars. She was great at pool, darts, and trivia. A queen of any bar she entered, she could handle her booze, participate in any bar activity, was sneaky smart, and had 99%

percent of the population wondering whether her boobs were real or not. They were real, and everyone including the lipstick girls were dying to see them. She pretty much wore the same outfit every night, jean shorts, boots, and a tank top. She would occasionally mix in a baseball hat or minimal make up on her porcelain skin. I doubt she ever had a pimple. She was naturally beautiful.

I love bars but I was becoming bored with the after hours scene, the passing out of people on our couch until the afternoon, too coked out to go anywhere or do anything, so I began straying with other women.

Danielle was one of them. She was eighteen on the cusp of nineteen when we started hooking up. I was a very lucky man. She was classical Liz Taylor beautiful, and smarter and better read than most of her professors.

She wrote me a love letter that convinced me beyond a shadow of a doubt that the stars were aligned in our direction, and I believed her. She was right. It was an easy call. My mom was quite fond of her and Danielle had a lot of respect from my sister and mother. She was basically forced to raise herself at a very young age.

Danielle's stepfather sexually molested her and her sisters and brother when they were children. Her mother was a drop-out hippie who either was too oblivious to give a fuck or she was complicit. Either way, Danielle came to live with her stepmom who was divorcing her father. He did a runner and took off for Japan on the Granny's dime to learn jewelry (zero presence emotionally or financially). The only thing he brought back was a young, pregnant Japanese girl from the woods who did not speak a word of English. Not much love or help from either parental direction.

Danielle worked full time at a flower shop and was a hostess at a Mexican restaurant/bar that Julia and I used to frequent. Danielle was also up for Valedictorian at her high school.

Plain and simple Danielle never let anything get in her way and just kicked ass, much like my mother. They both would have been right to blame their situations on others, but they just kept trucking. Pure motherfuckers!

I washed my hands of Julia after a particular night when we were out late at an after hours party. A girl who would hang out with us when her ex watched their two children, a six and four-year-old, decided at 5am that it would be a good idea to keep the party going and get in her truck and drive to see her dealer boyfriend and get more drugs. This particular weekend, the ex-boyfriend flaked and she was left with the kids.

Nearly two hours had passed, and another beer run had been made when someone mentioned she was taking longer than usual. Maybe she was getting laid. "Not with that limp coke dick boyfriend of hers," someone said. Then the phone rang; she had rolled the Jeep.

It was her on the phone saying she thought she was okay, but the police were arresting her and taking her to hospital to check her vital signs. Two hours later, the phone rang again. She was gone. She was bleeding in the stomach and there was nothing that could be done. She had passed and the party still went on.

Someone thought to call her parents and they came and got the kids. A memorial would be held for her, and fundraising for the kids would be held at a local bar where we all hung out the following day. You would think someone in the crew might think to hit the pause button, but it didn't happen. They kept on after memorial but I was over it already. I was off to Danielle, finished with the scene and with Julia.

Julia decided it would be cool if they partied after the service, so they went on getting more party favors. I had one foot out the door already with Danielle. I could not wait to escape the trap of that scene and run into her arms.

Julia was not going to go easy. She knew my sister and Danielle, and was a friend to both. She was also the best friend to my best friend's girlfriend, Nikola, and she loved the after hours scene- the bars and bands we knew. It would not be a clean break.

Nikola was the main bartender at the bar where everyone and almost every rising/established band would show up and play. The bar actually made it into *Rolling Stone* as one of the great bars in America. The crew including Julia made life extremely uncomfortable for my sister and Danielle, so they ended up not going to avoid confrontation. Instead, they would hold after hours of their own and soon the crew followed; what a mess.

The first getaway attempt did not go so well. Julia pulled out long scissors and began stabbing our leather couch, threatening to do the same to herself if I left.

The second attempt culminated in her caving in the door of my brand spanking new Cadillac. It was a punishing kick with her cowboy boots. She was not nicknamed Big Red only for her hair and natural DD tits that she suppressed with her custom red bras from La Perla just showing enough strap outside her tank tops or t-shirts, but she also had legs as long as

a Valentine's Day red rose.

73

The Yel

Friday nights at Hollywood Park were special because I would show up like Hugh Hefner with tons of girls around me and everybody wanted to get in our business. Only the patrons did not know how little money we had. One thing I learned was to never reveal how little or how much money you have. It doesn't look good for you either way.

That's when Jean Luc (aka JL) arrived in our lives.

"Come down to the paddock and I'll show you guys some horses," he said. What a thrill for me and the girls and everybody gawking. Getting that close to a race horse is exhilarating; they are such beautiful animals.

"Bet my horse here," he whispered.

"He's 89/1, a giant longshot," I said. *No shot to win* I thought to myself.

I wish I had bet more. Like a train, the horse flew down the stretch and passed the other horses, he won easy.

What a party and orgy afterwards. The girls were extremely happy, they didn't have to work the entire weekend.

They had bet some of their own money themselves, and then tackled me right near the winner's circle. We got a bunch of blow and there I was with goddesses all weekend long. Fucking, drinking sangria, and doing blow off my cigars, it was lovely.

The girls were rotating baths doing blow and drinking champagne, a true trifecta. And so began the mercurial relationship between JL, Neville a trainer I was friends with, and myself.

My dad would later get a piece of the action too. Here is how it went down. Neville, the other trainer, asked me if I knew JL. It was Saturday, a few weeks later and a Grade One race worth 700,000 was scheduled. JL's horse was in it but it seemed to be in way over its head against more expensive horses with superior breeding. JL's horse cost $16,000, while the others averaged $400,000.

I went over and told Neville, a very prominent trainer in his own right, to go gamble on the JL horse.

"Get the hell out of here," he said. "Too cheap, he's 90/1, keep dreaming."

Two minutes and $35,000 in my pocket later, Neville rushed up to me and whispered in my ear, "Find out what the fuck he's using."

I was trying to fund a film. I had a good manager/agent, Ira. We met at Dan Tana's Restaurant and he had strong ties with one of the major studios. The plan was to make the film myself, then sell it to one of the studios through Ira. We were referred to him by the waiter at the time, then the maître-d', and now the owner of a famous Restaurant known worldwide.

Raising money for an independent feature film is not easy. I had to hustle money, so I told Neville I could arrange that. So began my friendship with JL.

I did not know how to train a horse. I had no clue what medication to administer to a horse. I barely knew how to ride one, especially a thoroughbred race horse, forget it. I did not own one either, therefore I had no license or business being around these creatures in their barns and where they train. The only thing I sort of knew was how to place a bet on them, although I have had some losing streaks that could prove otherwise.

It didn't take much to get me into the back stretch, just bring Danielle and a couple of hot girls with her and *voila*. A lot of doors opened. Please understand and appreciate the fools Danielle and I were. We were truly naive idiots, the both of us.

She was immediately discovered at a restaurant by a world class director who had just shot a film. He set up a special day for her to be photographed so she could be on the poster that had Hollywood's biggest A-list actor. Literally, weeks later her face was on the side of every building, billboard, truck, and bus stop across the USA. She landed the agent who now handles the biggest A-list actor under 50 in the world. She would later quit that agency.

Within six weeks and after only a handful of auditions, Danielle read and got the part in a big budget film. The rug then got pulled out from beneath her at the last minute, because the biggest producer/director had the part given to his daughter as condition of his agreeing to work on the film. "This happens all the time," the agent said. "It's Hollywood. Tit for tat, don't let it bother you. There will be lots of parts in your future."

Instead of listening to her agent, Danielle quit the agency, and she banked everything she had on being the lead actor in our project/film. That would solve everything.

I had met a girl who was friends with a two-time Academy Award winning writer and the director of one of the world's most timeless films. We had been hanging out at a bar together occasionally and some intimacy had taken place. I told her about my upcoming script and film and she said, "I know a guy that could probably help you." So she called him and we headed up to the Hollywood Hills to go party and, as a bonus, he would read my script. He walked me into his agency the very next morning. Instantly, I was negotiating the price of sale of my script.

I was told over dinner with two famous producers that I would be hired to rewrite or co-write two unfinished

projects, and the writer who brought me in would also be co-writing my script with me. I would not be directing. It was not guaranteed that Danielle would be the lead actress or have any part in the film. I inferred that there was a strong chance Danielle would be totally excluded. I also thought this decision would split us up. Our lives were about to change dramatically.

I told them that I needed 48 hours to think about it. After repeatedly being told by Ira, my manager, my family, and even halfheartedly by Danielle to take it, I turned it down. I was told immediately that it was the biggest mistake I would ever make. It pretty much was.

What the hell? I thought.

It costs Hollywood a minimum of $10 million to make an independent movie, and usually hundreds of millions more. So fuck it. I thought we'd do it ourselves and I'd raise the money. Hollywood can pay me at least the $10 million dollars.

How fucking naïve I was. Easier said than done.

I received some money to start production based on the script. Danielle was dancing and saving money, and I saw a golden opportunity with JL and Neville to make a true score and raise the money for the film.

I was in the back stretch when I saw a white Ford pickup truck pull up to JL's stable. A thick manila envelope came out, and the veterinarian and JL went into the stall together. I really could not make out what was happening, but I did see cash exchange hands and JL told me it was just Lasix, a bleeding medication that was legal in horse racing.

"This is what works for me," he said juggling syringes leading up to the race. As he walked the horse towards the track, he handed me $1000 and told me, "Bet this for me. This horse can't lose." The horse won easier than a workout, and we both made some money.

Now Neville was desperate and called me and asked me again and again, "What shit is he using?"

Neville was training for one of the biggest owners in the world who had deep pockets. He had at least 120 horses in training and a new crop of babies being broken to run coming his way. The owner was frustrated with Neville because they weren't winning the number of races they should be winning with the amount of money he was spending. He was bleeding money. Neville was about to lose his meal ticket.

I approached JL and asked if I could try a sample of what he gave his horses on certain days for certain races. $3000 later and the vet in the white truck was meeting us outside the grounds of the racetrack.

If you are caught on the grounds with those drugs, you'll be suspended for life. It is illegal to drug horses on race day with certain drugs. It is considered race fixing along with a potential host of other violations.

The vet threw them in a paper bag with three loaded syringes, then I was on my way to Santa Anita.

"I think I got it!" I told Neville.

I got to the Burgundy Room, the bar that me and Neville used to frequent almost nightly, do blow, give away tons of blow, drink, and have sex with various girls in the bathroom over the course of three or four years. I even had a fivesome once! Over a couple a years, I must have hooked up with at least five hundred women there.

It was a tiny, candlelit dark room that only spun vinyl and periodically set the bar on fire by pouring kerosene or 151 then lighting a match. What a joint!

On one strange occasion, I ended up back at the SLS Hotel with a girl who would not tell me her name. She had several security guards walk us in, watch the door, then escort me home in the morning. All she wanted to do was get fucked, drink champagne, and send me on my way. I did not argue; what sane man would? I did find it curious that she insisted on doing it literally on mounds of jewels. It was an uncomfortable experience.

Neville was already at The Burgundy Room waiting for me; he was usually late.

"Do you have the paper bag?" Neville asked.

"Yeah," I said.

"Give it to me!" he demanded. I said no. I wanted to see what happened for myself.

"Fine," he said. "Meet me at Santa Anita tomorrow before the third race near the finish line, and let us see what happens."

I explained what JL had told me and instructed him which syringe went where. The thin reddish one went into the leg, the thick clear one into the throat.

"This is not going to come back dirty?" he asked.

"No," I said. "I wasn't sure, but JL told me to tell you to hit the throat last." As soon as he did, the horse's dick fell to the ground.

Neville looked at me. "Holy shit, did I kill him?"

"Beta blockers I think," I said.

"Who and where?" he asked.

I had to keep this secret. Being the middleman, I needed the money because I was trying to make a film. I didn't want to get squeezed. If I revealed my source to Neville or anyone I might not be needed. I had to keep myself relevant

to the task, be straight with the money, and keep a bit of scratch for my time.

The race was run and this horse won really easily, just like the last one. In regards to the owner with deep pockets, Neville was going to want more, a lot more, $100,000 more.

I figured I could make $25,000 in the exchange. I was on my way back the next day to Turf Paradise in Arizona, with $100,000 cash stuffed in my cargo shorts, and scrambled in what looked like a laundry mess in the trunk of my car. JL needed a few days to put the deal together; half in the front, half when he delivered. I milked an extra $5000 for myself.

Who better than my dad to drive back four boxes of needles in his truck to Santa Anita? It was perfect. I paid him

$10,000 to do it. Zoom! He was on the road back to Santa Anita that morning. At 4:00am he was to meet Neville after training at a breakfast spot near the track.

One of my first jobs as a kid was a newspaper boy. Rain, snow, or shine, at 4:30am every morning I would have to get up, fold, and rubber band the newspapers. Sundays were the worst, and Wednesdays were coupon days. Those were major hauls. I would stuff the papers in bags and hop on my bicycle and deliver them on my designated route. It usually took a couple of hours.

My dad hated excuses, whether for a poor performance during a baseball game or any sporting event, or a job. Just get it done and do not gripe about it.

We lived in a neighborhood with a lot of hills, and usually the weather year-round was pretty good. It was usually pretty cold and foggy in the mornings, but when it rained it was extra dark and a real pain in the ass. I also had to put the papers in an additional plastic bag so they wouldn't get wet.

Throwing papers in the dark on a bicycle during lightning and thunderstorms while dodging cars is not exactly a picnic. Most of the time this is where my father would shine. Sometimes he would beat me out of bed. He would get up with me, make me some hot toast with peanut butter and honey or molasses and hot coffee, and help me bag the papers. We then would put the papers in the back of the truck and he would drive my delivery route with me.

We would haul ass. I would jump out and grab five or six papers at a time, deliver them, then jump back in the truck. I wore big plastic trash bags that I cut to fit so I would not get too wet.

What would take two and a half or three hours on my bike took us about 45 minutes in the truck. When we finished, Dad would take me to our favorite breakfast spot and we'd talk about anything. I could eat whatever I wanted and never felt I was being rushed or pitied. We just took our time and weathered the storms outside.

There was my dad in a truck, right on time again, with boxes of God knows what, delivering them to Neville. Loads of syringes. Neville tipped him a G ball. "A thousand dollars will make you holler," he said. And all was good.

My dad was truly amazing, he was a great father. He did a great job raising us as decent individuals. Aside from the gambling and lack of financial acumen, he was a pretty good example to his children. He taught us great morals and values, drilled into us that we should never judge anybody by the color of their skin, race, or creed, taught us to play with everybody including the handicapped and special needs, and except for a few absentee years during and after the divorce, he was always there. Maybe not financially, but at least he picked up the phone and visited us when he could.

As far as gambling goes, he never messed up a wager. Well, maybe once or twice. But he was honest, right on time, and always correct with the money. Between all my girlfriends, filming, odd jobs, and even living in Hawaii briefly where the state does not allow gambling (they even track your IP address), he ran thousands of wagers for me through the years. He would get a cut of the winnings if I won. If I lost, there was usually still something in it for him. But the racetrack was a pretty likely place to find him. That's the primary reason why I would later leave Hawaii. No gambling allowed on the island.

I went there with a princess from the Philippines, of Spanish and French blood. Paulina came from a very wealthy family connected both politically and socially. Her mom was a self-made entrepreneur who moved up the class ladder quickly. They had several homes including a 26-room beach compound with servants, chefs, maids, drivers, and helicopters. She tolerated my gambling and affairs, and always told me, "Either I take or leave it, baby" with a Sobranie cigarette dangling from her lip and a glass of wine or champagne in hand. She was a tremendous chef and lover; she remains a good friend. Occasionally we will see each other when she visits the mainland.

Her mom and brother bought Paulina a beautiful penthouse in Oahu just south of Diamond Head on the beach. It was about a ten-minute walk into the city, Pink Hotel, Outrigger, the main Strip, etc. So it would be easy to find trouble whenever I wanted some alone time, to hang out at bars and meet girls on vacation. It was easy to get an invite up to a hotel room from single women on vacation from other countries and the states, watching other couples celebrate their honeymoon or anniversary and frolic and be romantic all day in the sun.

Paulina loved the island life, and was ready to retire at a young age (her family allowed her access to some of the money she would inherit). She wanted to enjoy the beauty of the islands and travel. When we left for Hawaii, I really was not ready for the easy life.

It was a rather abrupt departure. I still had a lot to discover and dreams to be fulfilled and unfinished business with the film and possibly trying to make another one. I had also just hit a small jackpot gambling the day before at Del Mar, my favorite track, and the greatest place in the world to be every summer. We left for Hawaii the day after opening day at Del Mar.

There is no gambling on races in Hawaii via phone or internet or off track. I was not aware of this. I probably would have stayed a couple of weeks in Del Mar then joined Paulina later had I known. I found out the hard way after landing in Hawaii, trying to get a bet down on the internet. I was denied. My prior vacations to Hawaii had just been for a few days, so I had actually relaxed and enjoyed myself and did not think about gambling. This was different.

I was on the phone to my dad within fifteen minutes. He held some money for me just for cases like these. He answered immediately and I was giving back daily donations to the ponies. A losing streak that wouldn't stop. The sickness never stops.

I am tickled by the notion that gambling is not a disease. Gambling does not define a person but can wreck one.

A late punter of mine who passed away from lung cancer once shared something with me. He said the other problem with gambling is that you cannot publicly overdose on it. It sounds absurd, but he's right. You don't black out like you do if you drink too much alcohol. You don't get rushed to a hospital because of code blue situations that sometimes happens with opiates and cocaine. It is a solitary suffering. You run out of money, family, and friends. Nobody has pity for a gambler like they do for a junkie. It is the most brutal form of self-torture.

At least with drugs and alcohol, you can share the misery – and the temporary highs – with others. If a gambler wins, they hide. They know how fleeting that high is and how briefly that money will last.

I have always been beyond generous with money because I know it's better for me to give now; I do not know when my next score will happen or if it ever will again. Gambling money has no home, no matter the bankroll size. It all burns away.

I will argue it is the worst of all the diseases and easiest to hide, until you are broke. The high never gets old. When people see gambling, they see only the winners. The jewels, private jets, stretch limos, beautiful women, lights, glamour. Monaco, racehorses, Kentucky Derby, hats, gowns, champagne, mint juleps, Langhe and Sohn watches. World Series of Poker, million-dollar jackpots.

There *are* winners. But to make a living at it regularly is difficult. What money and from whom do these palaces get built and grow? Why the red-carpet welcome at the casinos? Vegas is not an accident but a certainty. The odds are clearly against you. Society does not give the pity to gamblers that they do to other types of addicts (drugs, alcohol). Everyone feels sorry for them and gives them countless programs and chances. Where is the same consideration toward a person with a gambling problem? Degenerate is the most common adjective used to describe them.

There is no glory in being an addict. Broke gamblers pick up all the other bad habits and addictions.

If gambling alone was the only curse. They would gamble their clothing if it was all they had left. And that, and usually large debts and a broken limb, and/or homeless stories are all they have left. Almost everybody abandons them. It's a lonely disease.

I know many people who are drug addicts, my brother included. Once, on his way back to another rehab facility, he decided to jump out of the taxi on the 405 freeway near the airport. I was chasing him on the freeway during a traffic jam before the Century Blvd. off ramp, weaving between frozen traffic. I tackled him then muscled/dragged him back to the taxi. My brother still had a place/option/roof to go to. Broke, homeless gamblers do not have those same options.

I thank God for 24-hour restaurants and Korean spas that allow you a little comfort if you can hustle up a couple of feeble dollars. God forbid you fall asleep in the casino, the security or police will escort you out after your second snore. The very place that took all your money and dignity, and they'll kick you out in a heartbeat.

■■
The Yell

Pops was always too available to get down a bet for me. On time, no fucking excuses! He did this almost daily. He did it until the day before my family put him in an Alzheimer's home. It was an act of love and they meant well and it probably was an eventuality. My dad fought going into any senior care home tooth and nail, and so did I.

Jesus! He was still driving to the track and making countless bets for me, even though his mind was slipping. I do concede that occasionally he would get lost, but he was not ready for that home and I was not ready to accept that was the only option.

Meanwhile, JL, being the idiot he was, blew the easiest gold mine ever bequeathed upon an individual. He succeeded in giving us a fucked-up batch of syringes. Some were good but some were just food coloring. There was no way to know, so it was hard to effectively use them. How the hell was I supposed to know?

What a disaster! No more money from Neville, no more deals for JL, and eventually it was practically back to square one for me and Danelle. But that was wearing thin also. Famous actors were throwing money at her, and my sleeping around and bringing girls back home was starting to lose its luster.

It was when she got home late one night and saw me in the act with one of her best friends without her that the end was upon us. She still joined in, but the next day I was scolded. Our little house of cards and cookies and gingerbread was rotting and starting to crumble.

The movie had become a mission. It was our only hope. Financial dreams and us! And somehow, we managed to stay in love, until a month before shooting our film. And then shit hit the fan.

We had managed to get enough money to begin shooting. Like the stupid idiot I was, I decided to shoot the film on super 16 millimeter, one of the most expensive format mediums on earth. I was influenced by the Mike Figgis's film

Leaving Las Vegas and saw how he made that movie on Super 16. What I did not realize was how expensive the sound was. The sound is not married to the film and you have to go through a very expensive telecine process to sync the sound. Sound is the most important component in making an independent film; it is why many independent films don't get picked up or get finishing funds. Once you try to sell a film, if your sound is fucked, you're fucked too, and no amount of money can fix it, especially when you're on a budget. We were not about to go down that path.

We spent nearly $10,000 a day on the sound for the film and we got that shit right.

About three months prior to casting, I was looking for a co-lead for Danielle. It is not easy to find a girl with a ton of talent that would be naked for most of the film for little pay. We were determined to do an accurate and real look at the underbelly of what happens in and out of strip clubs. We wanted to show what these girls really go through. The real brutal world of stripping, not the one where Julia Roberts gets saved by a billionaire Richard Gere. Stripping is not a pretty profession for 99% percent of the girls.

It required me to have two other actors who were to be in the film, strip, and audition in real strip clubs and also work for a week or two at various joints to see what it was really like. True method acting. I wanted them to work on the slow nights to see how rough it really was, and on some of the busy nights to see the lure of why girls get caught up in it.

On Friday and Saturday nights, it is easier to make money. Working days and working slow nights gave these girls heart. Danielle worked somewhere well-known, wore wigs, and I didn't tell a soul. We told everyone she was doing data input for a law firm. Only our friend Christina from Arizona would cover for us. Christina covered for me and was my accomplice through three separate girlfriends, until she became so close to Danielle and my sister that she couldn't do it anymore. She told me she had had enough of my shit. She also was secretly in love with Danielle.

When Christina first moved to LA and did not have a place to live, she stayed in the hotel room with us. She would watch us fuck and some touchy feely. We were too close. I think in retrospect, everyone thought I would end up with Christina or Danielle or both of them. I wound up with neither.

Another favorite bar of mine was a small room that was basically a hideout for artists and some famous people who didn't want to be seen. It is also where I met Danielle's co leading actress, and probably another true love, Jacqueline.

Years later I began meditating, and during a class I fell asleep and started snoring. The teacher, who I had a massive crush on at the time, came over to me and woke me up. I went again once more but what was the point? I had fallen asleep at the wheel. And at about noon the next morning after waking up in Jacqueline's arms, I got the speech from her. It is either her or me.

I also got the same ultimatum from Danielle, after she witnessed the chemistry between Jacqueline and I. She grabbed my crotch again and told me, "I don't care where this goes but this is mine," then she banged my head with their fist and said, "Quit wasting your energy on others!"

Good advice that I never learn. I was asleep at the wheel on both counts. I told Jacqueline that it would be impossible to leave Danielle. I told Danielle what she wanted to hear. Little did I know she was planning her own departure with a very famous actor/athlete. She was also presumably in the middle of an affair because the tabloids were starting to follow her, taking pictures, getting weird calls, and our apartment was packed to the rafters with flowers. It was a very prominent athlete she would later tell me, and they were having a liaison together. I was oblivious to the life crumbling around me, too occupied with my vices and impulses to know what was really important, people who you love or can love and the possibility of accomplishing a goal.

I have eventually learned to stick to your gut. I lost a possible true love with Jacqueline and Danielle all within about six months. Like I said, Danielle and I held on temporarily and we started shooting the film.

Jacqueline had found someone else and started flaunting it in my face, on and off set, and what is scene it was. I was the maestro, and what a circus it turned out to be. You try getting 15 strippers to be on time for consecutive days, not paying them much to be naked, and being there by 12 noon. They usually sleep until 4:00pm for crying out loud. To their credit, they showed up and the tension between Danielle and Jacqueline was great.

I was starting to believe that we might have something special in this film. Hell, Danielle and I were even happy again. I think we both thought our dreams were coming true.

■■

The Yello

I must have had sucker written all over my face when I met Eden. We met at one of these back-alley speakeasies off Sunset behind a trash can, behind the building, through a secret punch code, a revolving brick wall, then down a tunnel. The place was a secret palace. We went into the elevator and up to a gorgeous private penthouse party. Everything was on the house, except for the blow which was served by naked waitresses. Tips filled the trash cans full of cash.

I do not kiss and tell, and I will not, but admittingly there were some major money players there, plus plenty of famous faces. And it was instant attraction between me and Eden.

I'm a sucker for women with glasses, and after immediately getting out of the way that we both were living with someone else, Eden and I hooked up repeatedly for weeks. We were having a blast. She planted the seed. She had a friend who could help me finish editing my film. Her friend had his own studio and had won a couple of Emmys. It sounded great.

I got more cash together, then gave practically all the money Danielle and I had left to Eden to give to him. I dropped the film off at his dad's award-winning studio. I was in good hands, or so I thought, trusting his reputation as an editor I was rarely there for the editing process. I was too busy drinking and freaking with Eden, among others.

Weeks later, without much involvement, I got back a mess of a film. I had a disaster brewing if I did not fix it. But I was out of money.

Eden was on the slopes skiing, blowing herself and probably someone else, having quite the snow trip vacation in Aspen and up her nose as well on my dime.

Asleep at the wheel again.

And just when I thought things could not possibly get worse, they did. In desperation I was looking for finishing houses to help re-edit the film. I sent the poorly edited project to what I thought was a place that helped independent film producers. It was not. It turned out it was an independent online review service, and the next thing I knew my phone was blowing up as a terrible review was on the Internet saying how awful and unfinished the film was. It was a total torpedo job!

I went out late that night and tried to tell Danielle it would be an easy fix. It probably would have been with money and a good publicist, neither of which I had.

We were having fun, and a girl wanted to join us later in the evening toward closing time. We went home that night and had a threesome with the girl. Danielle left me with the girl in the morning and said she was going to Christina's. I told the girl goodbye, then me and my friend Prince Victor, yes *that* Prince Victor went to the racetrack to try to make some money to save the film.

That should have been the sign.

The Yellow

Prince Victor was considered to be the all-time kiss of death at the races. The unluckiest gambler anyone ever knew. My first encounter with him was when I was coming up the escalator on to the mezzanine at the Del Mar clubhouse. I heard him before I saw him. There was this man in his mid-sixties, between 40 and 75 pounds overweight, bulging out of his clothes, in a cold sweat with an obvious brown hair dye job pouring down his cheeks. He was on his knees screaming to the sky, "Fuck you, God" for letting me bet on these fucking pinhead jockeys every day, you sadistic motherfucker! "Why do you have such a hard on for me?"

Trainers and gamblers would give him money to bet on the other horse they thought could beat them, this happened at least twice a month... In one case, where the most prohibitive favorite in horse racing history was running (meaning it could not lose), there was a gambler who was alive to another horse who had no chance under any circumstance. The gambler had called out the wrong number by mistake. The gambler gave

Prince $400 to bet on the prohibitive favorite, the horse that could *not* lose. The horse took two steps out of the gate and broke his leg. Prince pulled his dick out and went ballistic, screaming at the top of his lungs, "God, suck me! Only I can stop that motherfucker." The everyday fan, families, and "upper crusters" shrieked at him with horror.

He had to be removed by security. "I don't give a fuck," he replied. He was banned from the racetrack for two weeks. He was so sick as a gambler and as revenge, he dressed as an older woman and snuck into the grandstands and infield where the *Joners, stoopers* and super degenerates hung out. Security rarely patrolled these patrons, they were always broke digging for tickets in the trash cans or on the ground hoping someone accidently threw away a winning ticket-it occasionally happens.

Prince Victor would walk through casinos while other people were playing cards at the tables with their food trays next to them, right in the middle of their hand while they were betting their money away. Victor would put his grubby fingers in their plate and go "mmm mmmm" and grab their food. It was fucking hilarious. If the player looked disgusted or the pit boss got pissed off, he would just help himself to their food regardless. What could they do? They weren't going to stop playing cards in the middle of the hand and piles of chips on the table. Prince Victor knew the pit boss would compensate the player for the food and just yell at him or ask him to leave for the day. There was always another casino down the road open 24 hours a day.

There is a quote from a Borges poem that I think describes a gambler or addict very well. It could be argued that it's philosophically about anyone's life. My interpretation is, "Do we become what we have forgot, or do we forget what we have become?" El olvido que seremos... The forgetfulness we will be...

What nobody recognizes is that it takes great courage to be a gambler. You lose 90% of the time at the races or cards and losing another race or hand or sports wager is another kid's savings down the toilet. Yet you are right back at it the next minute until your pockets are dry.

Tough beats, all the "I almost won this much!" stories. And they still go back for more no matter how much mental torture the defeat wrought.

It takes a brave soul to walk through those doors and place a wager with rent money, food money, 401k money, the kids' college funds, the IRS, your paycheck! It is a brutal, sick addiction, and nothing, I do mean *nothing* beats the adrenaline rush.

It is also a very lonely sickness. You eventually see drugs, pills, and alcohol. But gambling as the root cause? Not clearly as much. It leads you like a blind dog walking into a swimming pool with no one to stop you. The gambler keeps kicking until they have drowned.

I still think great sex with someone the first few times is a little bit better. But you can always count on a gambling rush, a cannonball through a hurricane.

Once on the way home from the track I noticed Prince Victor was dangerously close to being out of gas. He always drove his car that way to save the extra twenty or ten bucks for the track. Pretty much every sick gambler does.

We left the racetrack and I pointed out to Prince Victor there a gas station a mile up the road. "CTFG" he said to me, meaning "challenge the fucking gods." We almost got over the hill then down the hill on Barham Drive to the gas station then suddenly there was a sputter, then another, then the final rattle, we were out of gas.

"Fuck you, God!" he screamed. Of course he had no gas can. I decided to walk to the gas station about a mile away. I got there with no money and no gas can, but left my ID and they let me borrow a gallon of gas in a gas can and Prince Victor and I came back to fill up the tank on one of his credit cards that worked.

I went inside to find a credit card that worked, fiddle around a bit, and got some munchies and a couple cans of beer. It was a slow-motion movie when I walked outside.

I came out of the mini mart and the sun was setting to the west, making it difficult to see. I saw the people staring in the same direction and then I heard him before I saw him. "Look what that god damn cock sucker has done to me!" he yelled.

I saw the gas pump flowing gas into the street. It was stuck and had fallen out of the car. The gas pump in the lock position was like a garden hose laying the curb and flooding the street.

"Prince, you got to get it!" I screamed. I saw the meter at 200 dollars. "Get in the car!" he yelled back at me.

"What about your card? The gas meter?" I asked.

"Fuck it!," he said. "That man upstairs has been fucking with me since the day I was born!" I got in the car and we drove on.

The other warning sign was Christina. She and Danielle shared the same birthday and sign, February 22, Pisces. I now believe that shit matters.

I met Christina in Tempe at a small, legendary rock bar. I was relatively new in town and the bar had been recommended to me by this cool rocker bartender girl at the hotel where I was staying. I had befriended the guitarist of one of the up and coming next great rock bands who had just been signed to a big record label. He approached me as I was standing on the perimeter of the crowded bar waiting for a drink. Over the loud music he yelled, "I need to pack my beak."

"What?" I asked.

"Blow. Can you find me some blow?" he said.

There she was, a random girl with her back turned to us, with gorgeous black hair down to her ass. She was wearing a floral dress and she turned to us and she was beautiful with Korean and German blood. "I can get it for you!" she said.

The guitarist, Bobby C and I looked each other, and asked, "What do you need?"

"500 dollars," she said. "Then meet at Nita's." It was a random bar off a dirt road.

We handed her the money. "How do we know you won't rip us off or even show up?" we asked.

"You don't," she replied.

"At least give us your name," I said.

"Christina," she said, smiling and scooting away.

Bobby C and I went back to the bar and shot some pool and waited. We watched a warm up band then waited some more. We watched another band and we were getting drunk. It was close to last call.

"Fuck it," I said. "You win some and lose some. Let's play a final game of pool and get out of here." I start to rack and in through the door at Nita's came Christina with a girlfriend named Belinda; they were dancing toward the pool table. Like marbles they started flicking little plastic bags of coke onto the table.

For the next 15 years through different boyfriends and girlfriends we were almost inseparable. I used to think that we would always be together: Christina, Danielle, and me.

Even after Danielle and I broke up, we still did everything together. We were a family, mafia like, one could postulate. It was pretty tough to get into our inner circle. We had our run of Phoenix and LA. Quite a few people wanted to be around us, and always wondered about our business. That is not conceit; it's just fact.

Two beautiful girls who can take down any room, especially Danielle. They seemed to always attract other beautiful, smart, and eccentric people. But we never kissed and told or called the paparazzi, we were just down.

Danielle and I were living at the Grafton Hotel on Sunset when we convinced Christina to move to LA and live with us for a while. Christina was always in love with Danielle. I think she loved me too, but she was also my best friend, confidant, and would get me out of trouble and defend me and lie for me through several girlfriends. I actually think she enjoyed it until I hurt Danielle one too many times.

I helped get Christina a new car, she gave me her old one, who I gave to my sister whom she had not met yet. The two of them later became like sisters. I stayed with Christina when I was on my ass with whatever girl or whatever situation I got myself into.

I look back on all the sworn pacts, all the nights up together and after hours, all the early mornings crawling out of bars, all the people we breathed in and breathed out, and never did I think Christina and Danielle would be so scant or absent now. Neither one of them had kids, nor did Christina end up with Danielle.

She still hangs a topless black and white photo of Danelle in her living room next to her authentic Neil Young and

Tom Waits photos from the Diltz gallery where a friend of ours worked.

It has been three years since Danielle and I have spoken, unless you count the one time she called when my father passed. She did not go the funeral. Danielle adored my father. They knew so much about each other. They would share their frustration about me as well as how much they both cared for me. They both knew I was wasting energy gambling and on spongy people who sapped me of my energy. They took road trips together back and forth from Tempe, Vegas, and Los Angeles. My dad moved Danielle and my sister's truck and storage to Arizona when they were 18. Heck, Danielle would run to the horse races with him to hustle deals and make bets.

I did not go to Danielle's wedding in which I was in on both sides, bride and groom, strange but true.

She called me and told me she was breaking up with Larry. I begged her not to. She and I occasionally fooled around through the years, but she was an adventurous girl and had been involved in several affairs.

She was currently in an affair with a guy back home every time she went to see her sick grandma. Larry was not very sexual. He was a heavy drinker who sold wine for a living. Larry was also very smart and interesting and we became friends. Hence, I was a groomsman on his side and whatever you want to call it on Danielle's side.

She wanted to call the wedding off. To this day I will never know why she pleaded with me not to let her get married. Maybe, just maybe she hoped I would get my shit together and get her back. We were as close to best friends as there is. Maybe she just was not ready.

Years ago she got pregnant three different times and we lost the baby on each occasion. One of the times she was pregnant and might have had it, we were engaged. It was an ugly miscarriage.

She was young enough to have children but developed a hormone problem that rendered her infertile. She was devastated and I was always there.

It was years before she became very ill. She got a bacteria in her blood that nearly paralyzed her. Maybe it was from food or water, but it was bad and she was debilitated and bedridden for months. I literally helped her piss, poop, and eat, and I carried her everywhere during that time. A lot of her so-called friends barely showed up. She would not have wanted them to see her that way, but she was comfortable with me.

I hope she still knows it, but she means a lot to me. I am in debt to her. She sacrificed a lot for us and was kind and generous to a great many people, even strangers she didn't know. My gosh, she went and gave Prince Victor's 94-year-old bedridden mother a manicure and pedicure; she spent the entire day with her. Danielle certainly had many stellar moments of grace and humility and I will always be grateful for that.

I actually got great satisfaction out of helping her. I did love her, and there is something liberating about devoting yourself to someone else on an unconditional level. I thought it was what we had, unconditional love. Time will eventually tell, God willing our health holds.

I've got to admit it does hurt me we do not communicate now. Unless someone close to us or one our old crew dies or has a major emergency or problem, we don't speak.

I did not get home until after last call, so I figured Danielle had gone to work and would not be home till 4:00am or 5:00am, because she worked a late shift, so I went to bed. When I woke up, she was gone. I started looking and noticed a few of her favorite dresses and shoes were missing. A couple of duffel bags and the money in the jar was missing too. She was on the road to somewhere, anyone, or anywhere else.

Out of money, Danielle was done with us, and my professional and personal life was heading to new lows: Korean 24 Spas to sleep, flop houses and all-nighters at any 24-hour restaurant I was near. Sofa sleeping and the floor of anyone who would have me were becoming too familiar. I was weak, pathetic, self-loathing, not worth two dead flies, and blaming everyone except the real culprit, myself.

When my dad was put into a home by my family against my wishes, it was very tough on me because I was in another city and state. He was in a place where I did need not to be seen for a while. I had just gone through a very dramatic relationship and breakup with Laura after Danielle. I did not need to see or run into this particular person again. I had no control of myself around her and would probably end up back with her. It took me a lot of time not to think of her.

I would dial the first few digits of her number and then quit, over and over again, several times a day, never dialing, not even drunk. It helped me to slowly ease the pain of the breakup.

My visits to my dad were limited, but we talked daily about everything, he still had his personal phone and we talked like he would be still running horse bets for me. We also talked about women, my brothers and my sister, and current events.

I would confide in him my problems about anything and he would listen and sometimes offer an opinion, or just start a new subject as if he had heard nothing. It did not take a genius to figure out this awful disease was starting to eat him up. Occasionally there were glimpses of his old self. I think he hated me for allowing my family to put him in that home.

I felt guilty not taking him in my care, but I was living in Los Angeles in the middle of three major boulevards. There are buses flying by every five minutes and the last time he drove here, shortly before they put him in the home, it took him four hours to get from Pasadena to Santa Monica, a trip he had made several hundred times before. Los Angeles was probably not the safest place for him to stay.

It took a few years for me to accept the reality that the film was not going to be the answer to everybody's dreams. I was tired of hustling money, an annoyance again and again to my mental well-being and self-esteem.

I had to get a job, only I hated punching timeclocks, nor did I want to be seen as a failure in the places where I knew people and hung out. I probably would have gotten hired had I asked. I had to get humble. I got a job tossing pizzas and bussing tables for a corporate chain. Nobody I knew would dare walk into a place like that, much less dine there. People in the entertainment industry, friends, trendy hipster wannabees, wouldn't be caught dead there.

Fuck! That was hard work! Rolling and tossing dough and bussing tables. Just to add to the agony, the pay was horrible. I had to make more money, take a chance, and go into commission sales. The only problem was I had not worked a regular job since I sold cars in Arizona with my brothers. That started well but did not end so good.

I had no clue about cars, none… yet I was quite good at selling them. My first month I made nearly ten thousand dollars.

The second and third months I was their number one salesperson. I literally knew nothing about any car. I would show up at 1 or 2pm and leave by 6 or 7pm then go out to the bars.

I wore shorts and an untucked shirt and wore my hat backwards. I was really pissing off practically everyone there, except the owner who said, "It's about time someone has hair longer than I do." Then he'd laugh. He was an ex rodeo/bull rider who became a billionaire in the car business.

I met a coworker there and we became quite serious. Brenda was the first and sometimes only person to show up in my times of need and friendship, though at sixteen she was the one who was left behind.

Brenda was always there to help with my father and any issues. She remains a great friend to me. When she was sixteen, she was making breakfast and her single mom went to the store and never came back. Brenda was left to raise and financially support her two kid sisters, ages four and eight, while she was going to high school. To the amazement of many, she did it. She and her sisters would joke about making a reality series called "Meet the Bastards" about their family. I still think it sounds like a good pitch to me.

We would later break up because of my gambling, financial irresponsibility, and occasional infidelities. We would try to make it work a few times down the road, but I just could not get my shit together.

I was doing whatever the fuck I wanted at the car dealership, and making more money than the nine to five sales pros wearing a suit and tie and knowing everything about the cars inside and out. I figured these customers already knew what they wanted, had done all their research, so I should just be nice to them, promise them a good deal, and stay the fuck out of their way.

We had a system where the salespeople would stand around then race down the stairs to greet the customer. First one to greet got the customer. You had to be sly. It required shrewd execution because of the makeup of the car lot. The general rule was not to have a mob of people running down the stairs and scare the customer away. Being that the average temperature in Az is 95 degrees seven to eight months a year, and 115 the other four or five months, we would wait on the mezzanine in the shade. When a car pulled into the lot, the first salesperson to the stairs would get the customer, or up as it was called. If you made a mistake and blew your chance on calling it, or being first, you had to wait three "ups" before you had your chance again.

What was the ideal up? A crew cab truck with six people stuffed in it. You knew that they were sick of squeezing in and needed a bigger car, possibly two. Or a middle-aged couple in about a four-year-old car looking to trade up. Best of all were the "Snow Birds," elderly couples from cold parts of the country who moved to Phoenix during the winter months. They'd drive in their cherry cars in exchange for the new model.

What not to waste your time or energy with? The one-legged up. A husband or wife by themselves looking for a brochure. Total rookie mistake running after them. One rarely buys without the other's consent. A wasted turn.

The tent sales were a total festival of fun. It was awesome working with my brothers. It reminded me of my father taking us to the tire store that he managed. He taught us to change tires and mount them on vehicles. It was early on Saturday mornings for a few hours, then he would take us and a few of the other people that worked for him to a late breakfast. They were all ages and we would hear their stories about drugs, concerts, and women problems.

We felt grown up and important, and I do not believe any conversation was off limits.

The tent sale was also the end of my brief car sales career. My brothers were always designated to run them because they were the quickest and best at making car deals on the fly. Once for a trade in we took a cow instead of a car. Another time we took a tractor. That client cried as we pulled up his new Cummings Diesel Truck.

The tent sales were also an excuse for coworkers to hook up in minivans, trailers, and the backseat of just about any car or truck. How do you like that new car smell now? It was like going to Vegas. There was a lot of cheating on spouses and significant others.

There were new clients too. Getting a new car can be exhilarating. I remember three girls buying a Jeep from me and riding back to their home with them. New clients took us to dinner and out for drinks. Shenanigans like these happened all the time.

My brother Antonio would have a line of women waiting for him. Name an excuse to come by and they did. "My blinkers don't work."

"How do I move my seat back?"

"Where is the four wheel drive shift?" Easy pickings. Might as well as said, "How can I fuck or blow you?"

Every tent sale there and every late shift at work meant coolers of cold beer hidden out of customers' sight. Sometimes the customers would insist on a beer or drink at a nearby watering hole before they made a decision. Curious and unsatisfied women usually ended up in the backseat of a car or a hotel room nearby. Men, especially the married ones, usually wanted to go to a strip club.

The weather in Phoenix (as before mentioned and cannot be understated) is brutal between mid-May and Halloween, and don't let anyone tell you otherwise, it is one big 40 square mile asphalt suburb with no trees or shade. I fucking hate it! It is as least 105 almost every day in mid-June, July, August, and September it's about 125. Rumor has it they measure the weather at Sky Harbor fifty feet above the ground in the shade, meaning the temperature is even hotter than reported. The taxi drivers from Africa even say that it is hotter than Africa. To take it one step further, in a city where rain is a rarity, the valley of the sun has both its baseball and football teams play indoors. Even the scorpions come out at night in this desert.

This particular tent sale was over the Fourth of July weekend, one of the biggest sales of the year, and it was 127 degrees in the shade. The rubber just fell out of the car doors if you opened them. I decided to show up late at about 4pm after a brutal night of drinking.

My brother was calling me all day, telling me to get there because it was "busy." But I knew better. Two of my workmates called me and said hardly anybody was there, and they had not sold a car yet.

I rolled into the stadium complex and it was death. *Nobody* was there; all you could hear were the bugs swarming.

As I wondered through the parking lot, I saw a mother and daughter in her late teens wandering around. It was time to jump in. I was as smooth as ice after the Zamboni during intermission at a hockey game, it was so perfect.

We had the car they wanted there. I guessed the perfect payment they could afford. I even put some leg room on the rate for the finance department in case their credit was shaky. I had the deal written out and signed before we got into the tent, to get shade and water. I went to the desk/my brother manager with the deal. I was pulling bottles of water out of the cooler while three other salesmen from different companies had told me there had not been a single sale all day. It was the supposed biggest sale of the year, but not this time.

It was a great deal. Plenty of profit for the company. We had taken in the car as a trade in earlier and got a good deal on it. It was a well taken care of automobile, a gem. I would let my mother drive it. It was a fair price and within the customer's budget, and they were happy, the mom hugged me! But it is in my nature to fuck up, and that is exactly what I did.

There was a cat who lived next door when we were growing up; I was probably nine or ten years old. The cat would kill everything its size or smaller, sometimes larger- birds, squirrels, and mice. Sometimes we would try to save the wounded animal if it was still breathing but my dad said it was in the cat's nature to kill it and that we should just to leave it alone.

On one occasion the cat brought the smallest, cutest baby mouse home and couldn't catch it again. We found the mouse in the backyard healing itself but bleeding a little the next morning. The cat was gone, probably sleeping in a bush somewhere. We picked up the mouse walked it two blocks down the road and set it free. The mouse was running and we were happy and giggling that we'd done such a good deed.

Then, out of nowhere while we watched the baby critter run away for good, a crow swooped down and grabbed the mouse by the neck and took it away, gone for good.

I walked up to the front desk and flicked my deal at my brother and the other manager. "Full pop deal with all the fixings," I told them. "Perfect credit, ran it already. Done deal." Mother and daughter were tickled.

My brother crumpled up the deal sheet and threw it back at me. "No deal," he says, "until I say so."

"Fuck that," I said. I turned my back and headed back to the mother to get a copy of their licenses and finish the paperwork. Two steps before I get there, a hard tug on my neck jerked me back. It was my brother and he stepped in front of me and told the mother and daughter that the car had already been sold.

"I'll have another salesperson help you find you another vehicle," he said.

A total lie, a total sales block. I turned and punched him. Then he put his head down into my gut and plowed me over four tables. It took several people including the general manager to break us up. All this in front of other dealers and the customers. I was under no delusion that my brother could probably take on 99 percent of the population and pummel them. I was lucky he did not snap my neck. I was sent home.

A day later I was told I would be working elsewhere. Not good, I totally blew it. Where else could I go and make ten grand a month working 11 to 5? Calling it work was a stretch;

all we did was fuck around between customers. Once we dared a newbie/green pea to drink a gallon of milk in 120-degree heat for $200. A green pea is someone who just started working, when you're commission-only salary and go a few weeks without selling a car, you pretty much do anything for money. The sales desk knows that and gets people to do all kinds of crazy shit.

An hour later, the green pea was grabbing his stomach and threw up all over the showroom floor. That gag never gets too played. Everyone eventually gets desperate for money. It's a cruel world.

Commission sales taught me that, no sale meant no eat. Some places will offer draw against commission for a few months, but those are humane places for workers with an actual resume.

The next place I worked was as inhumane as it got. It was brutality. It was run by a guy who gave me the chance to make good money. I needed to make good money. I owed everyone money, had nowhere to turn, and was obviously in the middle of a lot of bad gambling and women choices. I was a mess. Nobody would pick up my call, afraid I would ask them for money. The only time my phone rang was because I owed money.

My mom had it, but still called to tell me she loved me, and the sporadic girls would call hoping I'd get my shit together.

I found a spot. $1,500 to $5,000 a week making phone sales. It was managed by a ruthless guy who quoted constantly "no will get you further than yes in this business." It was a boiler room with constant stress and negativity shoved in your face.

There was a girl who worked there who was seven months pregnant and he made her count out loud how many weeks in a row she had not made a sale, week by week, goose eggs and zeroes up to seven weeks.

Then he fired her. "Pack your shit and leave," he said as she left begging and crying with security helping her out the door.

There was a sales board that displayed how many deals you got for a week, and when your last sale was. I saw a lot of starving people come and go.

To his credit, he would hire just about anybody from all types of backgrounds and hardship cases. A few co-workers with PhDs from Ivy League schools mentioned to me, "We are all here because we did not make the best choices."

Former famous actors, musicians, addicts in AA and those not sober, homeless or sleeping out of a car or on a sofa, ex or fired stockbrokers including ones who lost their licenses due to their own shifty dealings were a dime dozen working in the room.

First and foremost, I could not believe it could be done. In a nutshell, the job was to get someone on the phone and get them to invest in an autotomized system that made stock picks for them for 10k on their credit card. Then you'd open an account with their brokerage for 25k on one call. There were no callbacks ever! You'd be immediately dismissed if you called back. Do not let them off the phone till you got the credit card.

As brutal as it was, it made me a better, tougher, person. My first 15 days, I starved, pretty much everyone else there did too. Then one day a total genius older Black guy they nick named "The Moment" got a deal on a four-hour grind phone call with a potential client. They were praying in Native American tongues together when he got the deal. As desperate as it was, and after all of us rooting him on, it was a sign of hope.

I actually took myself out to an outdoor market with what little money I had to my name, bought a cigar and a pint of beer, and celebrated as if was my own deal.

The next day I hooked somebody, called him back at 5am the next day and made $2,000. It is amazing how fast life can change, for better or worse. People you breathe in and out. Possessions that are acquired, lost, passed on, or taken. Life is for the living, I am grateful for the health to live it. And when you least expect something, it just might strike like a lightning bolt.

I met her while on a date with another girl. Edith would later become my fiancé. She came in to pick up a to go order of sushi while I was waiting for my date to show up. I noticed her immediately when she blew in with cannon impact. Stunning woman!

I had to move fast, and I did. Pleading with the attractive woman waiting for takeout for her phone number while telling her I was on a date. She thought I was crazy but told me her name and number. Edith was probably blowing me off. I still wrote her number down and a week later we went to dinner. We got cozy fast, then planned a road trip together.

I left Edith inside the sportsbook in Vegas. I ordered her a drink and told her to wait for my dad to show up, I was going to go for a quick swim at the Hotel Pool before I started gambling and drinking. I was to meet my dad there because he had some money stashed for me that I'd won gambling.

I told her different. She had no idea I was getting money. She already thought I was successful because I had a film out. She had no idea what a disaster the film was. Though I was told there were a few interesting scenes and moments if someone dared to make it through. Nor did she have any idea what I was speaking of on the drive out to Las Vegas. I was dictating to my dad over the phone while she drove. "Give me a dollar pick 4. Numbers 278 with 1256 with 89 with 289…"

The sequence is made of races where you must pick the winner in 4 successive races , miss one and you are out.

Box the 7 with 1, 8 for twenty…

Trifecta key : 6 with 1248 with 12489…

50 dollar exacta wheel 7 with all , then key 7 in back with the 46…

All of it gambling jargon.

Complex bets for someone supposedly diagnosed with dementia. Turns out he was already in the sportsbook while

Edith was waiting for me. She mentioned to me that this

younger waitress was flirting with this good-looking older

man and was giving him extra attention across this

casino. When she pointed this out to me, I told her that was my

dad.

■■
The Yellow Pi

The financial sky had fallen on us as a family, and there was plenty of Texas weather between my mom and dad because of it. (Texans know if the weather is stormy, wait an hour and it will probably be sunny, or it could be a tornado. It is always changing and unpredictable). My dad had lost everything due to gambling including the house and his job and partnership at the insurance agency. We were bankrupt with a massive tax lien. He took a temporary job at a liquor store where everyone in town went. It was there they could witness our family plight firsthand.

My mom took me to the church with her; she had me run in to see the priest. She had too much pride to face him. He handed me a box of groceries and fifty dollars to give to my mom. She had taken up a part time job as an aerobics teacher that paid her cash per class. We had nowhere to go and nowhere to live. It is a pretty grim fate when you pull up to your supposed new place and the landlord tells you to keep your furniture in the moving van because she saw how beat up and old it was.

In addition to the four kids, for a two-bedroom duplex.

A family of six, a mother, father, three growing boys and a 3-year-old girl.

I figured out where that fifty dollars went, and the silent explanation for the box of groceries with canned foods and instant meals.

We took up residency at a motel that would work with us on a pay as we went basis. It had a roof and we had each other. "It could be worse," my mom would say. "We got our health and be grateful." Dad said it would be temporary.

One room, two beds, and a pool on the outskirts of town. Not the safest place, but not the worst place either. Kind of like a truck stop off the highway when traveling. It is ironic. I love hotels and motels, and still do.

When we would pack the family into the station wagon together then take the 14-hour road trip to Texas from San Diego, it was always a treat if we could cut up the trip and stay overnight in Arizona at a hotel with a pool. We were pimping when we could do that. All of us really loved it, especially my mom. Rates during the summer run very cheap there because of the extreme heat. We found it to be a privilege to stay where the rich stay during the winter months because of the great weather during that time of year and we could swim all night until the pool closed. We were right back there splashing water when the pool opened in the morning before we hit the road again.

I am always amazed at how forgiving a woman is of a man, but a man not of himself. My mom ran out of patience. In many ways, my dad threw in the towel trying to reach for something bigger and better. He had tried and succeeded several times, but the gambling choked his aspirations away and he became content in what he wanted his life to be. He remained a good father but was limited financially. There were about 18 months when he disappeared and none of us could talk to him or reach him. He would call on occasion to check in on us, but nobody had a concrete answer about where he was. Maybe with another woman. Maybe a new life somewhere where he didn't want to be found. Maybe a minimum-security facility for tax issues. Maybe my mom knew and kept it a secret. I never got an answer and still don't know about that year and a half hiatus.

My mom had given him too many chances and she finally let go. The amusement park ride was over. She walked the other way this time. She had lost faith and was not intrigued nor thrilled anymore. Too many promises unkept. She was a beautiful woman. She still is. It was time for her to move on.

When I made one of my first scores gambling, one of the first things I did was move into a hotel. I felt safe there and privileged. When you have bad credit, several girlfriends, bill collectors, and bookies looking for you, it has its advantages, and for the better part of fifteen years, hotels and motels were where I resided across the country.

It began before my second or third fiancé, Big Red, when I broke down and the yellow Pinto picked me up. It continued through Chicago, Kentucky, New Jersey, New

Orleans, and New York. With tons of time in Phoenix, San Diego, and Los Angeles.

My sister usually has a big Thanksgiving every year. About a year and a half before my father passed away, most of my family was there except for my brother Antonio. Everyone including my dad, friends, and relatives was there.

Edith and I took my dad and my nephew for the night, to take some of the load off my sister. Now keep in mind we had no idea how to entertain two wandering men, a 17-year-old curious kid ready to go party with a fake ID, and a man with Alzheimer's, who was still in relatively good shape.

After both of them got out of the house to go for walks and look around the city by themselves, they got lost twice in the middle of Los Angeles. After the cats brought back rats, then birds, from their outdoor hunting, it was quite a visit for my nephew and my father.

The taxi ride from Pasadena to Santa Monica was its own adventure. The driver put on racing gloves and literally drove like he was in a race. We caught air twice, flying over potholes and bumps on the rocky pavement of Olympic. We went that route to avoid the traffic on the freeways 110 South and 10 West through the downtown corridor. We all laughed, but hung on for dear life on the white knuckled ride back. It was a dare devil drive back home.

My sister, bless her heart, had to entertain about nine other family members at her house. Needless to say, at this point, unless you had a mansion with a guard or a huge backyard, my dad belonged in a nursing home. He needed to be monitored full time. 99% of those nurses working with those Alzheimer's patients are saints. It takes a lot of work, truly it does. It also takes a ton of patience and compassion. Patients aren't all zombies. Some become violent or overly affectionate, irritable, insatiably hungry, will not eat all, or regress to their childhood.

When I went with my dad to visit my grandmother, I remember her holding a little baby doll and calling me son over and over again like I was a little kid. My grandma died from Alzheimer's and when our family (including Danielle) went I remember the caregivers at the funeral crying. It really touched me.

What was even more amazing was my brother Antonio. When we went up together to visit the open casket, he reached in the coffin and started rubbing her hand. He turned to me and nearly yelled, "She's gone, baby! She is gone!"

It's not my favorite way to view a person. I will not look at an open casket again. It leaves the last impression and I want to remember that person living.

My dad could be checked out of the home by us whenever we wanted, but it was real tough bringing him back. He was still smart enough to know he did not belong there. I continued phoning him often and pretended we had the same thing going on. He loved to ask what types of music I was listening to. He had great taste in music. Too bad I cannot play a lick.

Some months passed and it was time to go visit. I had a crazy ex-girlfriend, or maybe I made her crazy, who lived near my brother. That is why I made myself scarce on visits to go see my dad. I would not visit him for months. I did not like seeing him in that home either. I needed to see him. I also needed to visit my other brother and his family. It had been some time, but I wanted to avoid running into her again. At least that was my excuse…

Once, my fiancé's daughter and I went to visit all of them for a few days and it was terrific. I saw a new side and perspective to what I thought was a very spoiled rotten Sara, the daughter of my girlfriend/fiancé Edith. She loved seeing my dad and hanging out with my family, my nieces and nephew, and their friends.

Sara grew up with no father present. Edith received no help financially, emotionally or anything from the completely invisible baby daddy. Edith worked her ass off to give Sara a better life, sacrificed her youth, joined the military, and her family spoiled the only child silly.

Edith is an amazing person, I am lucky to have her in my life.

Sara had a hefty addiction to Adderall, went to a prestigious high school with some very wealthy, influential, and famous friends, and was rather the opposite of her mother. She was also a little bitchy toward me and everyone else. Her nickname for me was The Thing, I am told. Some of her mother rubbed off on her. She was revealing and confided in me a great many of her personal problems, doubts, and

dreams, and we bonded. Sara was great with my family, I will always be grateful and remember that.

We danced, barbecued, played ping pong, and partied and my dad joined right in, taking it all in. It was seamless. It seemed like he was fine and just wanted to be part of the action and get some attention outside of the visits to the Alzheimer's facility by family. He was tired of the incessant phone calls pretending everything would be OK.

Then we had to take him back. I think the fact that he was so smart meant that he thought I was there to rescue him. I wish I did, or that I could.

We drove him back that night and walked him into the home. We went through the double doors to his room, then walked him in. He held me by the shirt and told me to wait. He was ready. He had packed all his clothes in a bag. He picked up the bag under his bed, then grabbed my arm again. "I'll see you later," I said. He knew better. Parents always know when their kids are full of shit. Especially a first born like me.

As I began to walk down the hallway toward the double doors with my dad clinging to my arm with his duffel bag. He clutched my arm so hard he left a bruise. I got to the double door and had to leave him. I could not look back. What a chicken shit I thought I was. Maybe my dad thought that his compadre, his best friend, his partner in crime was there to rescue him and take him anywhere but there. I cried my eyes out as I left and so did my family when I got to the car and told them. It would not be until about a year later that the guilt and feelings would only get worse.

The Yellow Pin

The Chateau Marmont called me, it was some bell man or concierge. I lived about a half mile up the hill from the legendary hotel in the Hollywood Hills on the Sunset Strip.

Laura had fallen or tumbled down the hill. She had no money to pay the tab or any ID on her. it was a complete mess. She was also beautiful, brilliant, and extraordinarily built. I mean she had gigantic breasts that defied gravity.

I called a taxi then went down to go get her. It was a very steep walk back up the hill. If you don't live in Los Angeles or are unfamiliar with the Hollywood Hills, one could get lost very easily. A person could also get exhausted navigating up the hills even in the best physical condition and knowing where they are going. If they get lost, they're fucked.

Laura had been drinking since she woke up. She was writing a novel. I was sure it was a masterpiece. I was not an editor, but had what I felt was a pretty good opinion when something great was developing. I helped her read aloud and gave her some thoughts about what may or may not work better.

I probably missed my one true love which is music. I cannot play or sing, maybe I should have been a talent scout. I can proclaim I have seen so many great rock bands before their time in tiny clubs and predicted their greatness too many times to count.

I felt like I was witnessing the birth of a generational author. It stirred me emotionally to be a part of it. Maybe I was too close. We started to follow a daily routine. We'd have very incredible sex bordering on dangerous. Then I would go swimming and people would stare at me with a look of concern. Those who knew me wondered. My chest and back looked like I'd been tortured. I was covered in bruises pinches, scratches, hickeys, etc. It was a side of me no one really had ever brought out.

Laura would sometimes make me duct tape her mouth because she would get so loud you could hear her orgasm or scream or punch or bang the walls or break things or whatever.

It sounded dangerous but it was not. It was so sensational, and I was all in.

I first met her in a bar in Tempe, AZ, and it was instant love for the both of us. She was leaving an abusive relationship, and I was there to take her away. And we flourished. We started every day drinking then having irreverent sex. She was a bigger girl, not petite, extremely pretty. And 30 pounds of her had to be her breasts. They were real. She was a lot of work.

Laura would start with a Shiner Bock then we would start writing. From late morning to long after midnight she always drank. It was a marvel to watch her do it daily.

I have been drinking daily since I was seventeen. I take the occasional day off to prove to myself I do not have a problem. But I run out of gas eventually and I put the pint or bottle down. I don't get completely shitfaced. I do have more than a few and maybe a few more. Okay! I do get obliterated on occasion.

I am definitely no lightweight. I can hold my own with the nastiest of alcoholics. My grandfather on my dad's side was a terrible, sometimes violent and demeaning alcoholic. He did not approve of my mother being of Italian and Spanish heritage. He was not tolerant of other races. My father taught us the exact opposite and led by example.

Once, to spite my mother who makes the best fried chicken I have ever had, my grandfather demanded I stay with him and he would make fried chicken. Staggering drunk he walked me to the chicken coup with an axe in his right hand, pulled out a rooster, and cut his head off on the stoop right in front of me.

"Pluck it," he told me. "Then we'll eat." He handed me the bloody decapitated rooster.

My dad told me repeatedly that if drinking changes your behavior toward violence or dramatic negative actions, stop it, manage it, or get help.

It was painful trying to keep up drinking with Laura, which most times I did. If no one told you your age or we did not keep track of birthdays, and god willing you were in good health, would you really know your age?

Some of the hippest, youngest, smartest, sexiest, and coolest people are definitely older than me and some are younger. I was trying to finish a screenplay and Laura had her novel. I had some money, but not a lot. We would head straight to the bar, then another, then we would close down another final bar to have the "final final" or last shot or last call. Oftentimes the bartenders knew us, and would lock the doors, so we stayed and drank more. It was routine.

One day we ran into a hideaway bar where Danielle had just gotten a job as a bartender. I didn't know she was working there until the moment we walked in. Danielle was wearing jean shorts and a black tank top; she looked good and fit. Laura was noticeably taken back by Danielle's beauty. Danielle has the ability to make one really welcome or irrelevant with a glance.

We came for the fish races, an odd drinking game where goldfish are dropped into a trough and squirt guns are used to move them into one direction, kind of like wiener dog races. It was instant hatred between Laura and Danielle which also caused quite a scene.

After a shot of whiskey and inhaling her beer, Laura pushed over the glass pitcher of beer and it broke everywhere. They started screaming and yelling at each other. Then a cat fight broke out. By the time they were pulled off each other, we were kicked out, and Danielle was fired.

Danielle did not take shit from anyone and we would be kicked out of some bars because she did not give a fuck who she offended, no matter the place.

It's why St. Patrick's Day became a yearly tradition at any one of our places, or at a bar where we knew the owner, or Christina's. Everyone would show up including current and ex lovers, a lot of magic on that holiday. We would Crock Pot the corned beef and lamb in Jameson, and boiled more corned beef, cabbage and potatoes in Guinness, enough said.

Strange partners, strange positions, situations, strange fights, and strange antics always took place. It is something you'd miss if you miss the event even once.

One time a girl balanced candles on her breasts and lit a fire on top of them. She molded wax on top of her breasts to make them stay upright. Word got out and a few girls tried to duplicate the feat, then it got dangerous. Coming down the stairs trying to balance the candles on fire, one girl fell and the tripped on the carpeted stairs. Everyone kind of stared then rushed to help the girl up. Simultaneously, a fire was quickly spreading. Someone grabbed the hose from the front of the apartment that we used to water the plants and drenched the fire. Thankfully, no one was hurt. The place was a mess, but the parties went on.

Sex and blow in the bathrooms and in public view. Drinking until throwing up rituals. Near overdoses and EpiPens and CPR would sometimes happen. Dicey near-death moments and sometimes deadly accidents also happened. There were fearful or unconscious moments, too many drugs laying around. Cocaine, heroin, opium, Molly, Vicodin, gummies/blunts, Xanax, and whatever else that alters your mental state. We were too paranoid to call proper help. Grand announcements and confessions ending with laughter, concern, or tears. I still celebrate it the same way, but these days most of the actors are different, or I am just alone.

The house in Los Angeles I was living in was located in the Hollywood Hills. There is a numbing, euphoric feeling to look down at the city and forget about all your problems like they do not exist. The view of the city is staggering at any time, but my favorite is evening, sunrise, or sunset.

It was summer in Tempe, AZ which meant it was 120 degrees every day, so I convinced Laura to quit her part time job and move to Los Angeles with me. We also did not need any more confrontations with either of our exes. Her ex was with a bona fide woman beater, a domestic violence perpetrator, a total low life scum, fuck him and all that. We were gone.

When we went back to pack the rest of her belongings, she had so much sex pasted to her, I wanted the scum bag to see and smell it. I told him over the phone to let her get her belongings and if she was not back outside in three minutes unscathed, I was coming in.

Laura falling down the hill was not a one-time occurrence. It became much more than an occasional event. Then it was weekly, then sometimes nightly. There would be fights or arguments with neighbors and the roommate, then the two of us having extremely loud sex.

Laura was either captivating or infuriating. She liked fighting or fucking.

My roommate was wealthy. He was a one-hit director who then dropped out of life over a woman. He kept a cake he had bought for her birthday- the day she broke up with him seven years earlier. It's probably still in the freezer.

Laura and I had to get away to avoid talking to him all the time. He was a very selfish person and only talked about himself and his problems. That meant more early day drinking for us. Hopping pools, room service, finding the early morning dive bar openings, wine and dine, and me running out of money quickly.

Soon the neighbors started to complain about Laura's antics. She had fallen down the hill again. The police even had to look through the bushes one night with helicopters, waking up the neighbors looking for her. But she was at her usual spot, The Chateau Marmont, waiting for me to pick her up and rescue her.

It was time for her to go, and I knew it. But I was near broke. Try to run at least a daily $200 bar tab for months and see how long you can last without working.

I booked her a flight without her knowing it, and I told her that we were going to the ocean for the day. Maybe we would go to Big Deans for starters, a place under the pier where they served tall cans of beer freezing cold and a great burger without it being a trendy gourmet place. It was revered among locals. Many of our pre-games started there then continued at Chez Jay.

We are heading south down La Cienega to the 10 West Freeway in a taxi and she was having a fit. I had told her I booked her a flight and was sending her home, not to the ocean, but I would meet her back in Phoenix because I had some business to do with my agent. She was not having it.

All of the sudden, bam! She had kicked out the window in the back seat. The driver slammed on his brakes. He got out and called the police. I got out and asked him, "How much is this going to cost?"

He held his hand over the phone and told me, "$600 and I'll hang up."

It was fucking blackmail. Perhaps I got off easy considering the danger she put us in while we were in a moving vehicle.

We flagged down another taxi and headed to the airport. It was imperative that she get on that plane and leave Los Angeles. As I let her out, she kissed me, then looked me straight in the eye and said, "I love you, I am pregnant with our baby."

Maybe it was the drinking. Maybe it was too many rolls down the hill, but after a couple of days of being alone at my room I was renting from a friend in Phoenix, Laura had lost the baby. I was on my way back to Phoenix.

I needed time, but I didn't have any. I was also out of money, and we continued to drown ourselves in alcohol, sex, love, and writing, but I needed to make a move.

Big Z was larger than life. Both as a man, and a personality. Nobody could miss him. He was considered one of the greatest pool and card hustlers since Minnesota Fats. "Introduce me to someone with an ounce of greed and I will take their money," he would say.

There were times he would tell me and whatever girls I was with (usually Danielle, Christina, and any handful of other girls) to sit in his supersized SUV and watch him in action collecting and exchanging money.

Big Z would stand in a parking lot of any generic location and at an exact time, a baby stroller would pull up, he would reach in the stroller, then hug the mother, then behind her back he'd show us a wad of cash.

Men in suits, women of all ages, other types of hustlers, club owners, lawyers, and people of all races would shake his hand or give him a magazine with cash stuffed in it. He loved to show us the cash while he was in action. It was beautifully orchestrated.

He would get in the SUV and have the girls count the money. He was very trusting of Danielle and Christina and even my sister on occasion. Zenith (aka Big Z) would then show us how to make a "boodle."

A boodle, is a big wad of cash that looks like a $50,000 cabbage roll, but it's really about three or five-thousand dollars mixed in with other bills in between Benjamins. It is truly an art to put one together. It's part of the hustle so one does not use all of a bankroll when looking for action. It's also used when a gambler is broke or desperate to get into a game as a high roller because it gives the impression that you have the money to play for big money.

I did not want to expose this part of my life to Laura. She knew very little about my gambling, just that I dabbled a bit with my dad. It was time to hustle up the troops and put on my dancing shoes.

"Just an ounce of thievery or greed in a person and I'll get them big," I kept hearing from Big T. He could smell desperation.

There was a private cigar club in Phoenix. A no-name joint behind the strip mall where PhDs and lawyers and the elite in the city would gather. A speakeasy happened every Thursday and Friday. The action for all types of gambling, sex, and schemes would take place. The place was always packed for card games, escorts, dice, pool, etc.

Sure, there was a Private Cattlemen's Club stuffed with loaded suckers to poach, and sometimes we did, but the speakeasy was better because it would always lead to something afterwards when the targets would start getting woozy and sloppy.

Usually the girls I would bring were a combo of Christina and a couple of strippers with Danielle, who would also bring beautiful girls to us. Even my sister would get in on the action. They wouldn't do anything illegal, just kind of flirt and see who was open to the pool, cards, and dice, then we'd pounce on the potential prey.

Big Z was cunning. He would just start half-ass rolling dice or shuffling cards or shooting pool and I'd give him the signal.

We did not always win, but we scored pretty much most of the time. Then he'd cut us off a piece of the take. I was astute to play along and lose some of the boodle Big Z would stake me with.

One night we ran into a big talker at Durant's steakhouse in Phoenix. He was with some friends from out of town who wanted a game. It was close to closing time and they didn't know where to go. I did. It was time to get the girls and call big T. He answered immediately!

It was Tuesday. "Let's meet at the spot," he said.

"Which one?" I asked.

"The spot," he said.

I knew which one, the speakeasy, but he just kept saying, "Come on, come on, come on, come on. No need to explain, see you in 45 minutes." We were on our way.

What a game it turned out to be! I got there with the guys and the girls would be there soon. They showed up and the minute they got there, I gave each of them $300 and they lost their tops immediately.

Christina made a pit stop at the dealer, so we had plenty of blow.

Maybe a few other lawyers stayed around, and we had about 15 topless girls and nine suckers waiting to get their money taken.

The night started poorly. The guys were up $40,000 in a hurry and they wanted to take the money and run. The girls knew what to do and kept them happy. They put on a happy face but that was just the beginning of their hot streak, and so the grind began.

Big Z got hot in pool and started to win some of the money back, but they were not biting. Cards is what they really wanted to play. They didn't want to play blackjack, they wanted to play Omaha. By the time the morning was nearly gone, Big Z miraculously found a card and took down $125,000.

When the smoke settled, we had cash, checks, and the title to a car.

Big Z was a very big man, 6 foot 7 at 420 pounds, not the kind of guy you would want to bounce a check to. He never carried a gun, as far as I knew, but kept one in the center console of his tricked-out massive SUV just in case.

I was off to Vegas to liquidate the car at my brother's dealership. The girls would meet me later.

Once, my sister's boss got out of line with her, drugged her up and she got scratched getting away from him, she escaped rape, but had revealing bruises. Danielle and I found her hiding in a bush after she called from the payphone upon her escape. She was rattled. I went to Big Z. We paid the guy an unpleasant visit. The guy left town and his job the next day.

Big Z flipped my sister the keys, then she and one of my girlfriends and Danielle were on their way to Vegas. My sister instantly wrapped the SUV around the tree. She could barely see over the dashboard and was not the greatest driver. She was fine and so were her girlfriend and Danielle.

I was not aware they wrecked his SUV until Big Z called me and said, "The damndest thing just happened in a parking lot. They're running late."

Big Z pulled another rabbit out of the hat. He got them into another car, and they met me in Vegas later.

My dad said never leave or quit during a winning streak, a lesson I should have heeded. Before I left for Vegas, I gave some money to Laura and we spent four wonderful days together. We had never been any more in love then in that moment. She pleaded with me not to leave and I told her it would just be some film business in Los Angeles and that I would be back soon. The girls came and went, my sister and Danielle after a few days, but I stayed. Why wouldn't I? I already had won six days in a row, I was getting everything comped and was enjoying the beautiful hotel by myself.

I was in love, but still had fun with other women. It was one of the happiest times of my life. Then, six days turned into 15 days and 15 days turned into 33 days. But I was a winner every day even if was as little as $50. The streak continued.

"Do not fuck with a winning streak," I kept hearing my dad say.

The calls mounted, everyone wanted me to come home.

My sister and Danielle showed up, again, I caved.

Laura was all too happy to see me again and for about six weeks, we enjoyed every moment together. I told her to quit her part time job and showed her the cash I had won. I was so in love with her. She was so incredibly intelligent and watching her finally finish a masterpiece was exhilarating.

I also kept working on a script that I was trying to finish, and I was helping her as much as possible with her book. I continued to give her notes and suggestions for rewrites, and I looked forward to every exciting minute with her.

My dad or Danielle would swing by and pick up money and sheets to make my bets for the day. My streak was finished. I had gone sour.

Pretty soon I had given back what I had won in Vegas with Big Z. I told Laura I needed to go back to Los Angeles for business. She wanted to come too. I would have said yes but I could not afford another place to stay. I needed money, I needed to roll up my sleeves hit the asphalt and to get a job.

When I was younger one of my most embarrassing situations was when my sister and Danielle were going through my closet to look for money and some drugs I used to stash in my pockets. They both found a little G-string, then went babbling to my mother.

When I was younger I auditioned to become a male dancer in front of this older blonde girl. She would call and give me assignments to go be an escort. It was a pretty embarrassing job for me for the most part.

I admire strippers/dancers/escorts both male or female. It takes guts and it's a lot of pressure to always perform or compete with other dancers for money. How far does one go to make that extra dollar? What does it do to one's self-esteem, relationships, tolerance, vices, and dreams?

It seems an easy way to make a quick dollar at first. It's something you'll do for a few weeks or months and then get out when you have made your money. But like gambling, it turns into years. In my opinion, it's a brutal grind to keep dancing for a long period of time. It's a hustle. Most times people end up breaking up with their significant others without much money saved.

Once, I went to a cowboy bar and there was a gigantic wooden dance floor. The DJ announced that I should go out by myself on the floor and dance, which I did to cheers and jeers. When I finished the routine, I had to go to a woman's table and dance for her with the cowboys cheering. It was very embarrassing. I ended up quitting, because one of my most dangerous situations occurred.

I went to go dance for a couple on their anniversary. A husband and wife answered the door. No problem, I figured. I thought he was going to watch. No big deal, that's exactly what he said he wanted to do. He watched his wife undress me. He was upstairs staring down at us on the couch. His wife takes out my dick and starts to lick, then inhale it. She then pulls me on top of her and shoves my cock in her and starts fucking me. I look upstairs and he was sucking on a gun in his mouth and jacking off. I got the heck out of there in my G-string, grabbed what money was on the table, then quit that job soon afterwards.

One of my most joyous situations came on one of the first nights I moved to Arizona. My dad helped me get into a cheap hotel. I had no car at the time, and I accidentally walked into a Mexican restaurant when it happened to be the Male Review Night or Chippendales night. I walked in at about 4:00pm, and after a few drinks the bartender looked at me at about 5:30 and said, "You're going to have to leave at 6:30 when the show starts."

"How come?" I asked.

He said, "The Chippendales come here and the women go crazy and no men are allowed."

"No problem," I said.

I had a few drinks, tipped the guy $20 and, then the bartender said, "Screw it, you can stay." Boy was he right, I almost got torn apart in there. I ended up bringing three women back to my hotel room.

I found out one of them was married. I have always had a rule about being with a married woman; it's the easiest way to get a bullet in your skull. I made her play with herself and watch, then I proceeded to have one whale of a night.

She was banned from my living situation in Phoenix. I just had to get out of the relationship as cowardly as it was.

I called my brother and told him to park two blocks away. It was another cooker day in the asphalt oven of a city as per usual, but I had to leave without warning.

Laura and I fucked like crazy then continued drinking Shiner Bock beers.

My brother texted me when he got a chance to leave his job, then said he would be waiting down the street.

She came outside with me and then I broke away running. She started screaming at the top of her lungs, "Don't leave me! Don't leave me!"

I paused about 25 yards down the street and looked at her one last time. Then she started breaking beer bottles all over the street. I yelled that I promised I would come back. It was quite the spectacle.

Then I started running as fast as I could. I hopped in the back of my brother's convertible and I was gone.

I called at least five times a day for three weeks. Promising over and over again that I would be flying her back to come and live with me. Then one night I got a video text. It was a picture of her with two black eyes; she had gone back to her ex.

It was the last time I ever saw her. I still think about her often.

I dialed her number repeatedly for months on end but never pressed send or called. I was too afraid I wouldn't be able to say no to any invitation she might offer.

I had found true love and was not up to the task of being in a responsible relationship. Too many vices.

It is often said that some people never learn. Maybe I am one of those people.

■■■
The Yellow Pint

"I have to pull over," the driver told me. Both windows were rolled down racing down the 5 freeway in a Scooby Doo Van. We had hitched a ride with him on Hollywood and Vine after The Cure concert when my friend Cole's car got towed away.

They were coyote smugglers. They made their living going across the border transporting undocumented immigrants and probably drugs and guns or God knows what else. They were on their way back to Mexico when they picked us up.

On the ride up, Cole and I had stopped and picked up Angel from work, then stopped at Kentucky Fried Chicken, where my youngest brother Raymond was working at the time and exchanged cars with my brother because his car worked better than ours. We took some chicken and biscuits to go, then started our drive up to Los Angeles.

As was custom, all three of us had a cold 12-pack of beer in the back and three Big Gulps half full of gin and half full of 7-UP. By the time we got to Santa Ana, we had to get out to take a piss. We stopped right off the freeway in a residential neighborhood where it seemed safe.

When we stopped, we noticed there was a party going on in the backyard of a house. It was only about 4 or 5:00 o'clock so we decided to sneak into the party through the back gate.

It was a huge party, a quinceañera. Nobody knew us so we stood out like a sore thumb; we definitely were not friends or family. We asked if we could use the bathroom and they graciously let us, but Angel was trying to pick up one of the girls at the party while we went back to the car to bring the remainders of our 12-pack in to share and be friendly.

When we got back, Angel was almost in a scuffle with another dude, the jealous boyfriend of the girl he was talking to. This was not a good situation so we pulled him off Angel and the next thing you know, we were running out the back gate. As we pulled away, gunshots were fired and one hit the trunk of Cole's car.

We pulled back onto the 5 freeway in a total panic and sideswiped a Mustang. We kept driving until we lost him. By the time we got to Hollywood and Vine to the Cure concert, we could not find parking and decided to pull right in front of the Palladium and park Cole's car alongside of the curb under the Marquee. We were from a small suburb in San Diego and we were awestruck in Hollywood. It never occurred to us that we could get towed.

What's the worst that could happen? They'd give us a ticket, big fucking deal, we never paid those anyway! When we got out of the concert venue, we noticed Cole's car was not there. We were stranded, which is how we ended up hitchhiking and driving with the coyote smugglers.

I looked in the back of the van and there were Cole and Angel wrapped in sheets, freezing to death from the wind blowing on them. I had a lunatic to my left driving the Scooby-Doo Van screaming at me, but he kept saying, "I need to pull the fuck pull over," so I told him pull the fuck pull over.

He pulled over, but before he pulled up his shirt sleeve and before he got out of the car, he started banging his right arm against his leg. I was like, "What the hell is this guy doing?" All of the sudden, he held his wrist bone, grabbed his fist, and twisted it back and forth. Then, a gusher of blood shot out of the hole in his arm in the middle of his wrist that was black and blue and rotted. It was a volcano gusher of blood onto the roof. It was one of the most scary and disgusting sights I have ever witnessed.

"I feel better," he said to me. We all get out of the car and took a piss along the freeway.

Sunrise arrived as we breezed through the border. I was thinking things could only get worse heading south to Mexico. So I told him, "Just drop us off on the next exit." Well, the next exit became the next exit, until the next exit exercise ended.

Finally, I demanded he drop us off in Ensenada. We were in Mexico.

"You got any money?" he glared at me. I thought we were going to die. I looked back at Angel shivering to death, he pulled $40 out of his left shoe and we gave it to him and the smugglers along with the first communion gold necklace that Angel wore around his neck.

My dad got a collect call at 7:00am from three drunk idiots, asking him to come pick us up in Ensenada, Mexico and take us back home to San Diego.

During our wait in Ensenada at some all-night underground cantina transgender whorehouse where donkey shows happened on the hour, the three of us continued to drink and Cole kept slamming shots. He decided to go outside and take a leak.

It all started in complete mayhem with a bucket of ice-cold beers then tequila shots were poured into our mouths by the waiters. They picked us up off the chair and shook us then blew several whistles loudly after we licked the salt and sucked the lime hanging upside down. It's quite a fiasco.

After about an hour, when we noticed Cole had not returned, we saw a policeman approach us. He said, "Your friend has been arrested and you need $5000 to get him out of jail."

My dad must have had ESP. It was not unusual for Cole to get fucked up beyond near extinction. My brother Antonio saved his life one night.

His nickname was Cole Quarters, he got better at any drinking game we played, then eventually things would turn to blackout phase. It was getting lethal when 151 Rum replaced beer and random shots.

It was late and he was missing from the party we were at. It was also winter and raining and breezy and for So-Cal by the ocean, it was cold.

"Where is Cole?" we asked.

Without so much as a whisper, like a flash, my brother ran and jumped into the deep end of a dark swimming pool.

Seconds later, he pulled Cole out of the deep end, gave him CPR, and brought him back to life. It was surreal.

Those same people who idolized my brother then, abandoned him later when he turned into an addict after being a freak of nature super hero type of athlete, a three-time All-American baseball player and major league baseball player just a few years before.

There was also the Denny's incident. It did not start there but that's where it ended. We started at some lunatic club/bar that had Tea Party Tuesday. There were all you can drink buckets of Long Island Ice Teas for a flat cover fee. Basically, it was a college bar themed night. Cole was shitfaced within a couple of hours, but our favorite live band was playing across town and we rarely missed them. Usually, we would drop Cole off at home then push on, but he insisted on coming. We were not three songs in when the bouncer tapped me on the shoulder at the table with my brother and a bunch of girls and

told me to get Cole out of there. He had pissed himself and was slumped passed out in the back corner of the venue.

We carried him into the backseat of the car and shut the door. We pulled out of the club parking lot. We drove about a quarter mile to make a U-turn and get on to the freeway. We heard empty beer cans jangle. I looked into the rearview mirror to make sure the cops were not following us for fear of drunk driving, then saw something moving around on the road.

My brother looked in the backseat and Cole was gone; he'd slid out of the car.

We doubled back to pick him up, got him off the street, his face covered in blood, and put him back in the backseat.

It was time to head home, but we decided we should probably sober up a little bit ourselves and let Cole sleep it off for a bit before we cleaned him up and got him home. We left him in the backseat passed out and snoring loudly. We put a couple of t-shirts under his neck so he was elevated properly; he just kept snoozing away.

We had just gotten our food, when in through the glass door came Cole, his face caked in blood. It was not pretty. He staggered from side to side, knocking into tables, spilling and breaking plates everywhere. He flopped right on top of the table. The manager rushed over and went ballistic, threatening to call the cops. We only had about 80 dollars between the three of us.

After pleading and begging with the manager not to call the cops, I left the keys to the car, my ID, and the 80 dollars with the manager, promising to give him 300 dollars within 24 hours.

My dad got another call to pick us up. We did not dare tell him what happened except that Cole was really fucked up and needed to get home. We scrambled up the money the next day, and thankfully moved on.

My dad made it to Ensenada in three hours. We asked the Federali where we could meet the cop to go get Cole. We met two police cars on some dirt road two blocks down the street from the bar. My dad gave him the paper bag of money and we got Cole back.

After he got us, he dropped everybody at their home with some bitching and moaning, rightfully so. Then he told us a few crazy stories about some of his buddies and lessons we should learn after he took us to breakfast. It was a pretty big ask of my dad, and a long trip.

My mother and sister would sometimes get these calls from us drunk lost idiots to pick us up. They would show up when my dad couldn't.

He always sounded angry when we would call him, and we knew it would piss him off, but he always showed up.

For my birthday, when I was about eleven, my parents got me the baseball glove I had wanted for years. It was expensive but I was getting good at the sport. Major League Baseball players whom I cheered for had the same glove.

After baseball practice the next day, I forgot my glove and left it at the community baseball field. It was almost dark outside when I told my dad. I was so ashamed and he was not happy to hear the news. He told me to get the flashlight and we went back to that field and looked everywhere for almost two hours. My brothers came and searched too. We did not find the glove.

My dad did not say a word. It was a silent ride until we parked and he asked if we wanted ice cream. He gave us some advice about being responsible for your own shit and owning up to it, then we went home.

A teammate of mine who had stayed late to practice returned the glove the next day. My dad would pick him up and sometimes give him a ride back home almost everyday because his mom was working two or three jobs at a time. He had no father. His mom had little help.

It was the only glove I would use over the next six years. I played baseball until I wore it out.

I remember the phone call from my brother. He said I had to come to Arizona. It was about my dad. He had maybe 24 hours to live. I was on my way.

I was working and I was and am still owed a lot of money by a weasel company with thieves for owners. I wanted to get paid before I left. But I didn't get paid then or ever. I hoped my brother wasn't overreacting.

He wasn't. When I went to go see my father, he was not well. I remembered when he stuffed $100 in my pocket and told me to go make a wager for him. I remembered when, as a kid, we would take our road trips to the grocery store just to get out of the house, or just go on long aimless drives to anywhere but home to have long talks.

I remember my dad piling me, my brothers, and other kids in his truck and driving to the baseball field or vacant basketball courts or any vacant lot to teach us to play a sport together. He was really cognizant of other kids' inclusion and having us have positive interaction with each other. Kids get in fights and arguments all the time, but I think it was important for him to let us work it out among ourselves. I think he gained this perspective growing up an only child in a scarcely populated small town off the highway in the middle of nowhere New Mexico. He was probably grateful to have anyone to play with.

I remember going to watch older kids in high school or college play sports, or fishing at the lake or the ocean, and music concerts at the parks, beaches or clubs.

We'd go wherever was free or what we could afford, just to be together. Going anywhere with me alone or with my brothers just to be father and sons. I didn't know how lucky I was, but I always felt special because of that.

It was not easy to see him the day before he died. He had had it. I think he refused to eat, and had just checked out, period.

It's obvious I failed to save him. He had given up any hope that I was going to rescue him from that nursing home. My sister was in the room with me while my girlfriend Edith waited

in the lobby. Edith took me there and was a rock; she has been a blessing in my life.

She had lost her father to pancreatic cancer when she was 20 and he was 51. She was with me during my father's last bid, and with me for my sister, when her husband died of pancreatic cancer at 52. Edith sill tolerates my gambling sickness and my occasional no shows. I have become a much better and accountable person because of her, but she still does not know everything, so we will see where it goes.

Loneliness is an epidemic in this world. During the death of a loved one it is exasperated.

My sister, a young widow with two children to whom I am a proud godfather will need all the help I can muster. My mother will be there too. When my sister's husband passed in his sleep, he had to have known he was loved. But let us be honest, when we die, or we are told we have limited time left, nobody can know how to process it. Loneliness is spreading faster than any virus in this world.

My sister and I listened to some of my father's favorite music with him and talked about current events and the horse races as if we were going to make plans to do it all again like it was tomorrow. He knew better.

He played along for a few hours, and then my sister left me alone in the room with him. I knew it was the last time I was going to see him. So did he.

It was strange. We kind of looked at each other and I pretended that it was all going to be OK, so I kept talking about baseball, music, sports, my girlfriend- who was still waiting outside the room, whom he met once or twice before, and liked.

Then all the sudden, he rose from his pillow and grabbed my arm in a vice grip. He said something in my ear, an undecipherable mumbling with a slight scowl on his face. I hugged and kissed him and told him I would see him tomorrow.

I think he knew better.

■■
The Yellow Pinto

The Yellow Pinto

B. WalterWill

For more info:

Online	www.theyellowpinto.com
Instagram	@theyellowpinto__
Twitter	@theyellowpinto
Threads	@theyellowpinto__
Email	read@theyellowpinto.com